Loved

RELATIONSHIP RULES FOR WOMEN WHO THOUGHT THEY KNEW THE RULES

Julie Shafer, PhD

hello@drjulieshafer.com

www.drjulieshafer.com

Ordering Information: Special discounts are available on quantity purchases by corporations, associations, and others. For details, contact the publisher at the address above.

Loved: Relationship Rules For Women Who Thought They Knew The Rules / Julie Shafer, PhD.—1st ed.

ISBN 978–0–9600091-0-7

Book layout: ©2017 BookDesignTemplates.com

Contents

For my clients
who bravely confront their truth
and discover they are capable of so much more
than they thought.

Before you speak,
Let your words pass through three gates:
Is it true?
Is it necessary?
Is it kind?

~Rumi

Introduction

FOR THE PAST TWENTY years, I have been working with women who struggle with a wide range of life issues. Despite their many differences, the one thing almost all of them talk to me about is their relationships. They all want to move beyond the hurts of their past and stop being afraid they'll never have a good relationship. They want to show up, be seen, and have a great relationship with a great guy.

I could relate. My first marriage ended after my husband refused to support my desire to go back to school. We both wanted a family, but I wanted a career, too. My second marriage lasted twenty years, but we were only happy for the first couple of years. He was out of work and we didn't understand each other, and as a result we were miserable.

After being single for two years, I decided to start dating. I wanted to set myself up for success. I wanted to move beyond the pain of my two marriages and have a great relationship with a great guy, so I made two rules for myself: First, I would own my emotional reactions and not blame my dating partner for how I was feeling.

Second, I would pay attention to and believe his actions more than his words.

As I paid attention to my relationships and helped my clients with theirs, I added more rules. Eventually, they coalesced into seven rules that made amazing things happen when I used them with clients. My clients started verbalizing their experiences, taking better care of themselves, and gaining confidence. They confronted their partners, made changes, or ended relationships. Along the way they gained self-confidence and self-awareness they didn't know they'd been missing.

These rules are about doing relationships in a healthy way. If you are unhappily married and practice following these rules, your relationship will change. If you are divorced or widowed, these rules will help you find a great relationship by making troublesome behaviors more obvious early on. In either case, the rules will help you conduct yourself with confidence and integrity.

The secret is as you practice these rules, you practice loving yourself. I don't mean the mushy-gushy feeling of falling in love or being in love, but rather the beliefs, awareness, and actions that show love and support. You do it for other people all the time. Now it's time to start doing it for you.

If What You're Doing Isn't Working, Do Something Different

YOU'RE MOST LIKELY READING this book because you are unhappy with one of your relationships. You want the kind of relationship where you feel supported and loved. If you haven't felt loved recently, it's natural and right that you would want things to change. I wrote this book to give you a way to make different choices about how you conduct relationships so you can have better outcomes. I want you to be happy, and this book will walk you through seven rules that help you be more honest, more responsible, and more compassionate toward yourself and others.

By the time we reach adulthood, we all have emotional wounds. There's nothing wrong with that, but they can get in the way of healthy relationships. Even if you are a rational, thoughtful person, your wounds may be clouding your perspective and driving your reactions. Reading this book and going through these exercises will help you become aware of your patterns and emotional triggers, as well as teach you how to talk about and change dysfunctional patterns.

You will learn to be truthful, especially with yourself. Being truthful is extremely difficult, even though it sounds easy. The difficulty lies partly in the expectations of how people should behave versus how they actually behave, as well as what they think and what they believe. Interestingly, problems with telling the truth result partly from our inability (or unwillingness) to handle the truth, but denying the truth only leads to more unhappiness.

If you look for truth, you may find comfort in the end;
if you look for comfort you will not get either comfort
or truth, only soft soap and wishful thinking to begin,
and in the end, despair.

~C.S. Lewis

Since the truth can be quite difficult to communicate, you will learn a strategy for assertive communication that will help you tell your truth with compassion and kindness—not aggression.

You will learn that being compassionate and kind does not mean you will get your needs met. Neither does it mean you will be taken advantage of. Many of my clients tolerate bad behavior from their partners because they believe they need to be understanding and agreeable to get their needs met. This mistake costs them their ability to stand up for themselves and leaves them vulnerable to being taken advantage of by their partners and others. The rules in this book will teach you how to be compassionate and kind while at the same time asking for what you need to be happy and healthy, even if it conflicts with what your partner wants. You will learn how to be compassionate while not tolerating bad behavior.

The rules appear in a specific order and build on each other. They start with the importance of telling the truth (Rule #1) to others as well as yourself, which becomes important in the second chapter on believing people when they show you who they are (Rule #2). Rule #3 discusses the importance of assuming the best in your partner in the absence of information to the contrary.

Rule #4 encourages readers to pay attention to their limitations, which is another form of being intentional with the truth. The limitations I outline span the physical and emotional and encourage self-compassion for those limitations. Whether limitations are the result of failing on our part or are the result of things that happen to us, there is no point in being overly harsh towards ourselves. We are better off learning how to take responsibility for our emotional reactions (Rule #5). Doing so will also help us better handle our partner's emotional reactions, something nearly every client asks about at some point.

Our emotional limitations are often the result of experiences from our past that intrude into the future. Our emotional brain wants to keep us safe and quickly recognizes patterns, even though the players in the pattern are different and will inevitably behave differently. Thus Rule #6 talks about recognizing past patterns and outlines the importance of using the other rules to take ownership of your reaction, be truthful, be compassionate, and communicate effectively so you can challenge ineffectual reactions and create new ones.

Finally, because there is an exception to every rule and because this book cannot cover every situation, I included a rule to guide you when the rules don't apply. Rule #7 is to be kind, which isn't necessarily as easy as it seems, just as the first rule is not as easy as it seems. This rule circles back to Rule #1 because being kind often means telling the truth, even when it is uncomfortable to do so.

These seven rules and the accompanying exercises are presented with an intention to guide you toward healthier relationships. The overarching themes of honesty, responsibility, and compassion are threaded throughout the rules and exercises. When you have finished the book and completed the exercises, even if you don't fully recall all the rules, remember these themes. They will serve you well.

Rule #1:
Tell the Truth
Sooner Rather
than Later

Three things you can never hide:
the sun, the moon, and the truth.

~The Buddha

Tell the Truth

IT SEEMS SO SIMPLE—tell the truth. We were all taught as children that lying is bad. But navigating the intricacies of any relationship is tricky and you know it isn't always as simple as just telling the truth. No one likes to be lied to, but people lie a lot. Some of the lies are little white lies and some are whoppers. The kinds of lies you tell and the reasons you tell them are varied. In this chapter, I'm going to cover ways people lie, reasons people lie, and what to do after you have lied. And because telling the truth is hard, I've included a section on effective communication.

Remember the oath taken by witnesses in every courtroom drama scene on television? "Do you solemnly swear to tell the truth, the whole truth, and nothing but the truth?" This simple oath covers all the ways we have of not telling the truth—three ways to lie.

Three Ways to Lie

The first type of lie is what you would call a bald-faced lie. It is covered by the first phrase of the oath: "tell the truth." This is your standard lie of "I didn't do it" when you did do it. The second type of lie is a lie of omission and is covered by the phrase "the whole truth." This is the lie where you say you went to lunch with a friend, but failed to mention that the friend is your ex-boyfriend, which would upset your current boyfriend. Finally, the phrase "nothing but the truth" covers those statements that aren't lies but are designed to divert your attention from the truth. This is when, rather than admit that you didn't get a particular task done, you redirect attention to three tasks you actually did complete.

Just as we have several ways to lie, we also have many reasons to lie.

To Protect Ourselves

We lie to protect ourselves from the judgment of others, the consequences of mistakes, and to avoid feeling ashamed. Have you ever said you had a headache to avoid having to go out? Rather than just telling your friend you weren't up for getting together, you made up a story that took the blame off you.

We lie for the sake of our own safety or the safety of others, whether physical or emotional. If you find that you need to conceal the truth to be safe, it's important that you recognize what you are doing and why. If you feel threatened physically or emotionally, tell yourself the truth of the situation. If you've been in this situation for a while, stop telling yourself the situation will change (see Rule #2). A substantial number of women across the world find themselves in situations where they are being controlled, manipulated, and abused. If this is you, I encourage you to find help. You can find a list of resources in the appendix.

To Manage People's Impressions of Us

This kind of lie is meant to give the liar a gain of some sort. For example, Bernie Madoff lied to his friends and colleagues for years to create a Ponzi scheme that pulled in millions of dollars to support his luxurious lifestyle. While his lie was a real whopper, it's not uncommon for people to engage in lies like insurance fraud, shoplifting and then returning the item for cash, or getting married for immigration purposes only.

People lie to give others a more favorable impression than the facts would support. Consider boasting politicians, spouses who have affairs, and people who set up charities to make money for themselves. Impression management is in play if you've ever blamed traffic when in reality you left the house late, if you've ever claimed you sent an email you didn't send, or ever called in sick to work when you just wanted a day off.

Sometimes people lie to fit in. We go along with our friends so we don't have to look like the oddball, defend an unpopular opinion, risk being ostracized, or risk being embarrassed.

Impression management is also important for people who are up to no good. They have to make it seem like they aren't the kind of person to do anything wrong, which helps others overlook their egregious behavior.

To Impact Others

People lie to impact others both positively and negatively. Have you ever failed to tell someone that the dish they brought to the potluck was bland, overcooked, or had the texture of sand? Of course you have. There is no point in making someone feel bad unnecessarily. We often lie to be polite—or at least to avoid being rude.

Occasionally we lie to help others. For example, telling a child that the gift they received was from an important person in their life who actually forgot about their birthday.

On the negative side, there are people who are malicious and lie just to hurt other people. This kind of lie would be lying to hurt someone's reputation out of anger or for a sensational story to tell.

Unknown Reasons to Lie

This category is saved for people who lie simply because they can get away with it or because they are pathological liars. Pathological liars lie with no apparent motive. They make up lies, sometimes quite elaborate lies, for reasons that are hard to fathom. At times it seems like they are not fully in touch with reality.

Everyone Lies

At the end of the day though, it's not a matter of being a liar or not. It's more a matter of how many and what kind of lies you told today. We tell lies to justify our behavior by telling ourselves we don't want to upset the other person, we don't want people to think poorly of us, and we don't believe we deserve to suffer the consequences of a mistake. We lie to our most intimate partners. We cover up the nature of a relationship with a co-worker so as not to hurt our partner's feelings. We may make up stories about slow traffic so we aren't to blame for being late. Sometimes our partners consistently do things to annoy us, but we ignore it because we think it's no big deal. However, after a while we realize that our annoyance is only growing and eventually we need to say something or it's going to come out in other, less controlled ways.

While there are many reasons to lie and we all do it at least occasionally, the fact is that concealing the truth about yourself or how you feel interferes with your ability to get your basic needs met in your relationships.

That's because lying will set in motion a series of behaviors intended to conceal the lie.

Carrie

Carrie's husband had an annoying habit of making decisions without involving her in the process. One year for their anniversary he bought and installed a closet organizer in her closet. He didn't ask her if she wanted a closet organizer and he didn't involve her in its design. He just bought it, gave it to her, and proceeded to install it, expecting Carrie to appreciate his wonderful gift and all the effort he'd put into installing it.

At this point Carrie had a decision to make. She could tell him that she loved the organizer and appreciated him for installing it. Or she could say, "Hey, thanks for the effort in picking this out, but I'd prefer to have something else." If she tells him she loves the organizer, she doesn't confront the fact that he tends to make decisions in what he believes is her best interest without involving her in the process. While this approach may risk an argument or hurt feelings, it gives Carrie a better chance of getting her needs met now and in the future.

Carrie told her husband a white lie: one of those little untruths or fibs meant to keep the peace. She said she loved the closet organizer; she didn't want to hurt his feelings. She could tell that he was proud of his idea and that it felt good to him to install it for her. He would be crushed if she told him she didn't want it—or at least that's what she told herself.

The truth is, she likely told that little fib because she didn't want to risk his disappointment, anger, or rejection, especially after he'd put in so much effort. Furthermore, she was avoiding the possibility that she would feel guilty for upsetting him.

White Lies

There is some debate about whether these "white lies" are really lies. If you think about it, you'll see that fibbing is a way to grease social interactions and keep conflict to a minimum. And it's true, white lies do keep conflict to a minimum. But they also separate you from the person you are telling the fib to. In effect, when you tell a fib, you are behaving as if the other person can't be trusted with the truth. While some people can't be trusted, you might be surprised at how well people can handle hearing the truth—at least occasionally.

What about the whoppers we sometimes get ourselves into? What about the developing relationship with a male co-worker who seems to just get you? Or your increasing use of alcohol to de-stress at the end of the day? Or the plethora of parking tickets your partner doesn't know about because you've been skipping out on work to gamble? And so on.

Tell the Truth

Even though being deceptive is common and everyone lies at least occasionally, it's still important to be honest. Be honest about how you feel and why you do things. Tell your partner what you like and don't like.

Express your opinion and point of view to the best of your ability. Do all this even if it makes you uncomfortable, even if you risk an argument, even when it makes you feel exposed.

Vulnerability and Intimacy

Telling the truth makes you vulnerable to the disapproval of others and their rejection of you. You become vulnerable to standing out and being judged negatively. You become vulnerable to being known as someone who is rude. It's hard to be vulnerable. But the amazing thing about vulnerability is that it is the part of us that other people can relate to. No one is perfect, and being vulnerable allows other people to see us as human and relate to us more deeply. When you make yourself vulnerable to others, you have an opportunity to experience greater emotional intimacy.

Telling the truth sends implicit messages to you and to your partner; messages you may not be aware of. When you tell the truth, you send a message to yourself that you are an honest person who has a valuable opinion, an opinion worth something. It empowers you in a way that telling a lie never can. In psychology this is known as self-signaling. It means that you judge yourself based on how you behave. If you behave in a kind manner, you believe yourself to be kind.

Telling the truth to your partner sends your partner the message that you respect him, that he can be trusted with your honesty and vulnerability. Respect for a man is very important; possibly more important than love. By telling him your truth—what you honestly think, feel, and believe—you trust him to handle you and your perspective with care and respect. If your partner is interested in pleasing you, telling him your truth makes that easier for him.

Sooner Rather Than Later

After Telling a Lie

As we all know, telling some truths is difficult, especially if you initially told a lie. Depending on the nature of the cover-up, coming clean can be a painful and regretful process. This is why you need to come clean sooner rather than later if you initially concealed the truth—or even told an outright lie. The longer the lie goes on, the more impact the lie will have on you and others.

Stella and Max

Stella and Max had been married for about seven years. They had a young son and a baby on the way. Stella worked in a hospital laboratory in a position she enjoyed and derived much satisfaction from. Max liked a more fast-paced lifestyle. He worked in radio and was a member of a popular band, so he was very involved in public appearances and promotions. Stella was content with her career and mom duties and wasn't part of Max's world. She didn't complain or talk to Max about her desire to have him home more often and to be more involved with their son. When Stella attended one of his band's shows and was backstage with the other wives and girlfriends, she heard one of the women mention Chrissy, someone Stella didn't know. When questioned, the woman reluctantly told Stella that Chrissy was particularly close to Max and there were rumors that the two were having an affair. Stella was crushed. She immediately left the show and went home. When Max got home, she confronted him. Max played it off as an unfounded rumor and told her that she was his only love. Stella wasn't convinced, but she was pregnant and scared of raising two children on her own, so she didn't press the issue.

Costs of Deception

One needs to consider the short-and long-term costs to being deceptive. In the short-term being deceptive is often beneficial—a conflict is avoided, you've managed the impression others have of you. Both Stella and Max engaged in a deception for short-term gain. Stella didn't tell Max about her desire to have him home more, because she thought he would be angry with her. The more obvious lie was the one Max told when he said the affair was just a rumor. Sure, they both avoided short-term conflict, but we all know this story isn't going to end well.

Lies like this can be quite costly when the deception is discovered. The longer Stella and Max pretend like everything is okay, the harder it will be when one of them becomes so dissatisfied that they walk out on the marriage. This is why telling the truth sooner rather than later is a good idea: it minimizes the long-term cost. If Stella had confronted Max in the beginning, they could have worked on their differences to get what they needed from the relationship. Ultimately it is easier to confront a truth early and deal with it when it is manageable than to wait until resentments build and the relationship is compromised beyond repair.

How to Tell the Truth

It's admirable to aspire to tell the truth, but relationships can be tricky, which makes telling the truth hard. It's especially difficult if you haven't been honest in the past. The question arises, how exactly do you go about telling the truth?

Why Be Deceptive?

The first thing we have to do is determine what makes you want to be deceptive. What do you hope or expect that hiding the truth will do for you? You can refer to the earlier section of this chapter on reasons people lie to help you figure out what kind of deception you are guilty of. Are you trying to protect or promote yourself? Are you hoping to get people to have a more favorable impression of you? Are you just doing it for fun or to manipulate others? I've included a worksheet in the appendix titled "Why Did You Lie" if you're interested in exploring this further. At the end of the day, unless you are lying to be manipulative or to harm someone, chances are you're concealing the truth or lying because you are trying to avoid a negative emotion such as fear or guilt.

What negative emotional state are you trying to avoid by being deceptive? Think about the situation and how you expect the other person to react to the truth. If he or she were to react that way, how would you feel? There is a worksheet for Why You Avoid the Truth in the appendix; please take a minute or two to do Step 1. It will walk you through a process that helps you identify how you expect to feel. Labeling our emotional reactions is a way of putting boundaries around something that is otherwise vague and limitless. Once you know what you are dealing with, it's easier to figure out what to do.

Challenge Your Expectation

If you did Step 1 of the worksheet, you have written out your truth and labeled how you expect to feel if you tell that truth. Now it's time to challenge your expectation of what will happen. Right now you are acting as if your expectation will happen. However, people are notoriously bad at predicting the future. Unexpected things happen all the time.

Ellen and Paul

Ellen began to work with me because she had come to the point of being willing to leave her marriage. Ellen and Paul had been married for over a decade, so she thought she knew Paul really well. The problem was, she was dissatisfied with their relationship and didn't expect Paul to be willing to make changes. Because she thought he would resist change, she was fearful of confronting him. She didn't want the relationship to end but knew if he didn't agree to make some changes, she couldn't stay.

We worked on how to talk with Paul. Although she was willing to entertain the idea that Paul might be open to her concerns, she was reluctant to believe he might respond positively. Despite her fears, she eventually wrote him a letter. She knew she had to express her concerns or nothing was going to change.

To her complete surprise, Paul reacted with openness about making changes and expressed some of his dissatisfactions, too. It was as if he had needed Ellen to express her concerns before he could express his. Now that both had aired their issues, they agreed the relationship was fixable and started couples therapy. This would never have happened if Ellen had let her fear of how Paul would respond stop her.

To challenge your expectation, ask yourself if it will be as bad or painful as you fear. What's the reality of the situation? If you have lived with someone for many years, you may believe you "know" how he will react. And, you may be right. But you may be wrong. People can and will surprise you, even if you think you know them.

Amanda and Phil

Amanda had been dating Phil for several months but he never asked for a commitment and neither did she. Then one day Amanda met Trevor and they decided to go out. Because she was not in a committed relationship with Phil, she reasoned that it would be okay. Trevor and Amanda had a great time, but the next day Phil called Amanda and expressed his dismay that she hadn't answered his call the evening before. Amanda had a choice at this point: Should she tell Phil she was out with Trevor or not?

If Amanda assumed that Phil would be upset or if she feared he would quit seeing her, she would be tempted to lie to him. On the other hand, if she assumed he'd understand since they hadn't discussed being committed, she would be honest with him.

If Amanda lies to Phil, until he learns of the lie, he's in the dark and ill-informed. He believes something that isn't true—that Amanda is truthful and trustworthy. Once he learns of her lie, that belief will be destroyed, which could destroy the relationship. It's a big risk. By lying, Amanda compromises her integrity and possibly loses the relationship, too.

If Amanda tells Phil the truth, Phil has a chance to evaluate how he feels and can make a decision about what to do. It provides the two of them an opportunity to discuss their relationship. They could decide to be exclusive, keep the relationship as it is, or decide to move on.

As it turns out, Amanda told Phil she had gone out with Trevor. At that point Phil realized he didn't want Amanda going out with anyone else and that he didn't have a desire to see other women, either. He expressed this to Amanda, and after talking about it, they decided to be exclusive and see how their relationship developed from there.

Now it's time to do Step 2 of the worksheet Why You Avoid the Truth. Step 2 is about imagining your partner responding differently than you expect and how those responses would make you feel. If you are having a hard time believing that telling the truth might not result in what you fear, check it out with a friend, family member, therapist, coach, or mentor. Talking to another person helps because it brings a more objective perspective to the situation. When we get emotionally embroiled in a situation, our thinking is usually not clear enough to be able to see other points of view. It's the proverbial problem of not being able to see the forest for the trees. Get another person to give you a different, more objective point of view. You might be surprised!

Why Knowing What You Want is Key

One of the factors guiding Amanda's assessment of whether or not to tell Phil the truth was whether she knew what she wanted. While we can always aspire to tell the truth, it's much easier to do it if we're clear about our desires, values, and goals.

Most people are aware of what they are afraid of and oblivious to what they want. If you are someone who has not had much practice at identifying what you want or getting what you want, then you may not know. Obviously, if you don't know what you want, then you can't state your preferences or ask for what you want.

You likely have a problem with knowing what you want if:

- You don't have an opinion about most things
- You find it easier to go along with what other people want
- You're too accommodating
- You've ever thought of yourself as a pushover
- You've noticed that others get what they want more often than you do

Rosemary

Rosemary's story is an example of an accomplished woman who isn't clear about what she wants. She was a fifty-year-old accountant who had run her own private accounting & bookkeeping firm for the past ten years. She had been single for the last five years, then fell in love and started spending time with a new partner. Inevitably, the two of them had conversations about moving in together. Rosemary told me that ideally they would move into a new place together, but practically it would make more sense if her partner moved in with her. During their discussions, her partner said he wanted to replace her furniture with his and do a little redecorating. It was during that discussion that Rosemary realized she tends to be too accommodating.

She had an uneasy feeling about her partner's proposal. Her furniture was a little more worn than his and her décor could use some updating, but she didn't want him to move in and start making major changes to her life. She was having difficulty telling him that, and she didn't even know why she was having a negative reaction to the idea. In short, she felt she should accommodate him, and she didn't understand her own reaction—because she didn't know what she wanted.

Does Rosemary's reaction sound familiar to you? Do you find yourself in situations with vague feelings and a sense that you should be accommodating to others? Do you spend time figuring out how to be okay with a situation rather than try to figure out what you really want? Have you ever thought that you are a pushover? Fortunately, a few simple changes can help you tune in to your reactions and find out what you want.

You Can Learn What You Want

The first place to start is with learning to have an opinion or a preference. Start with small things such as what you want to eat, what routes you prefer when running errands, your color preferences, whether you like the blinds up or down, etc. Look at items and conditions around the house and how you do errands and tasks. Ask yourself whether this is what you want. If you aren't sure what you want, experiment a little. Choose something to eat and ask yourself if it's what you really wanted or if there is something you would have liked more. Take a different route when running errands, observe what's nice about it, and then ask yourself when this might be a better route for you. If you find something that is not quite right, figure out what would make it better for you. The act of noticing what you want will start exercising the muscle of knowing yourself better. The nice thing about starting with simple things is there's no judgment, no right or wrong answer, no one standing there expressing a preference that creates in you an urge to accommodate them.

Now Go Tell Others What You Want

Once you are doing this on a regular basis, it's time to start expressing your preferences to those around you. Do you want your partner's help making dinner? Ask him to help you. Are you getting together with a friend for lunch and need to decide on a meeting place? Offer a suggestion first. Is your book club discussing the next book to read? Make your suggestion and/or express a preference among the books being considered.

As you do this exercise, be sure to state what you want, NOT what you don't want. A simple example of this is deciding what you want to eat for dinner. Rather than going through a list of what you DON'T want, identify what you DO want. Translating this example to a discussion with your partner, if the two of you are deciding where to have dinner, figure out where you want to go, rather than where you don't want to go.

It helps to be as specific as possible with your preferences. Being specific means being more clear about what you want; then when you express yourself to others, they are also more clear about what you want. For example, rather than saying you don't want your partner to sit on the couch watching television after dinner, say that you want him to dry the dishes you are washing.

Because you are asking for something specific, he has a better idea of what you want from him.

Once you start figuring out your preferences and expressing them, it won't be long before you have something more important you want to say: something that scares you, something you "know" will create a long discussion and possibly an argument. If you have a history of avoiding difficult conversations (which most of us do), then you're likely to feel like you don't know how to have the conversation. Let's remedy this problem by starting with a primer on effective communication.

Communicating Effectively

At its core, effective communication is about sending a message to another person in a manner that maximizes the chances they will receive and understand it. That might sound like a no-brainer, but it's common to forget that the way a message is sent can have a dramatic effect on whether it's received. Imagine that you tried to send a text message to someone who didn't text. Or imagine that you used a language the recipient didn't understand. These are obvious problems, but a less obvious example of sending a message the recipient "cannot" understand is sending your message when the recipient's emotions are triggered and they are defensive or angry. Sure, the words coming out of your mouth are spoken in a common language, the recipient can hear those words, and you aren't using big words, so the recipient "should" get the message. But the negative emotional tone of the conversation means the recipient is not hearing a word you are saying. We have all been in conversations like this. We know we are not being heard and our point is not getting through. It is frustrating to say the least.

To maximize the opportunity for your message to be heard, the message has to be delivered in a manner that minimizes the chances the recipient will be emotionally triggered. That is why it's important to learn how to communicate effectively so you can confront the truths you need to say. This is where an assertive communication style comes in.

Assertive Communication

Assertive communication is a way of communicating a message that recognizes the desires, feelings, opinions, and rights of all parties involved in the discussion. When you communicate assertively, it's easier for others to understand what you want and to support you. Let's contrast assertive communication with two other styles: passive and aggressive. The passive communication style is a way to avoid speaking up for yourself. When you use this style, you are taking the position that your desires, feelings, opinions, and rights are less important than the other person's. Similarly, if you communicate using an aggressive style, you are not taking into consideration the desires, feelings, opinions, or rights of others. To many people who are not used to communicating assertively, it can feel aggressive, but don't confuse the two styles. Being aggressive means you are not taking others into account, but being assertive is holding everyone (you and others) in equal regard.

Your Rights in Relationships

The biggest stumbling block my clients have had in learning assertive communication is overcoming common assumptions about their rights as adults in relationships. People have many assumptions that get in the way of expressing their desires, feelings, and opinions. Some assumptions are what they were taught as children, while others are "rules" they learned to avoid unpleasant interactions with others.

Some of the assumptions listed below are considered social norms—unstated expectations about how to behave. In some instances, following the social norm is the best option. But in others, the assumption should be challenged and your basic rights asserted.

For each assumption, there is a corresponding basic human right. You may not ascribe to all these assumptions, but take careful note of the ones you use and examine the corresponding right.

❀ ❀ ❀

<u>Assumption</u>: It is selfish to put your needs before others' needs.

<u>Right</u>: You have a right to put yourself first sometimes.

<u>Discussion</u>: People often use this assumption to avoid being "selfish" without giving much consideration to what being selfish means. They are trying to avoid putting themselves first at the expense of other people, but just because you put yourself first doesn't mean you've

done so at the expense of others. When considering whether you are being selfish, consider whether putting yourself first is costly to another person. Even then, it's not necessarily a bad thing to put yourself first. It's just one thing to consider.

❄ ❄ ❄

Assumption: If you can't convince others that your feelings are reasonable, then your feelings are wrong or unreasonable.

Right: You have a right to all your feelings.

Discussion: This is an interesting one. Your feelings are your feelings, and they are valid whether or not anyone agrees or understands. No one has the right to tell you how to feel or to negate your feelings.

❄ ❄ ❄

Assumption: People don't want to hear that you feel bad. You shouldn't take up other people's time with your problems. Keep it to yourself.

Right: You have a right to ask for what you want, including help and emotional support.

Discussion: While it may be true that others find it hard to hear when you are feeling down, those who care about you will want to support you during times of distress. This means you may need to choose thoughtfully who you turn to for support. Choose people who want to support you and who do a good job at it.

❀ ❀ ❀

Assumption: You should respect the views of others, especially if they are in positions of authority, and keep your opinions to yourself. Listen and learn.

Right: You have a right to your opinions and convictions.

Discussion: People usually learn this one as a child because someone in authority told them that children should be seen and not heard.

❀ ❀ ❀

Assumption: You should always be logical and consistent.

Right: You have a right to change your mind.

Discussion: People value consistency because it lets them know what to expect. Chain restaurants are popular because no matter which location you enter, you know what's on the menu and how it will taste. But people are emotional, and emotions don't care about consistency. Emotions care about what feels right at the time. This means no one will always be logical and consistent.

❀ ❀ ❀

Assumption: Other people have good reasons for their actions and it is not polite to question them. You should be flexible and adjust.

Right: You have a right to be angry and protest unfair treatment or criticism.

Discussion: While other people may have good reasons for their actions, that doesn't mean you have to accommodate them, especially if their actions result in unfair treatment or criticism of you.

❀ ❀ ❀

Assumption: It is shameful to make mistakes. You need an appropriate response for every occasion.

Right: You have a right to make mistakes.

Discussion: This assumption is a striving for perfectionism in order to avoid the pain of shame. Shame is ubiquitous; everyone has shame. Also, everyone makes mistakes. There is no getting around this one.

❀ ❀ ❀

Assumption: It's impolite to interrupt people.

Right: You have a right to interrupt to ask for clarification.

<u>Discussion</u>: While interrupting too much is disruptive and sometimes disrespectful, depending on how it's done, there is no hard and fast rule about it. People expect to be interrupted occasionally, especially to be asked for clarification. Sometimes people don't want to interrupt when they don't understand because they assume that asking questions reveals their ignorance or stupidity. However, if you are paying attention and asking a clarifying question, this shows that you are engaged and listening. People love to be listened to.

❋ ❋ ❋

<u>Assumption</u>: Don't ask for things to be different, because things could be worse. It's better not to rock the boat.

<u>Right</u>: You have a right to negotiate for change.

<u>Discussion</u>: While it may be true that things could be worse, that doesn't mean that the way things are is okay.

❋ ❋ ❋

<u>Assumption</u>: Be grateful for what you have, because others have it so much worse. Other people have problems of their own and don't want to hear your problems.

<u>Right</u>: You have a right to feel and express pain.

<u>Discussion</u>: Consider this scenario: If you saw someone get hit by a car and at the same time you stepped off a curb the wrong way and broke your ankle, does the pe-

destrian's more severe injuries mean that you shouldn't have your ankle treated? No. Your problems deserve to be addressed regardless of how they compare to other people's problems.

❀ ❀ ❀

Assumption: If someone takes the time to give you their advice or opinion, you should take it seriously. They are probably right.

Right: You have a right to make your own decisions regardless of the advice or opinions of others.

Discussion: Sometimes if you ask for advice and then don't follow the advice, people get quite upset. They interpret your behavior as disrespectful. But just because someone gives you their opinion doesn't mean it's the right course of action for you. It is important for you to gather different perspectives and then make the best decision based on your own unique situation.

❀ ❀ ❀

Assumption: Knowing that you did something well is its own reward. No one likes a show-off or a braggart. No one likes arrogance. Successful people are disliked and envied.

Right: You have a right to receive recognition for your work and achievements.

Discussion: There is a difference between receiving recognition from others for your hard work and being arrogant or a show-off. When people give compliments it feels better to them if the compliment is received graciously, rather than brushed off.

❀ ❀ ❀

Assumption: You should always try to accommodate others. If you don't, they won't be there when you need them.

Right: You have a right to say no.

Discussion: While accommodating others promotes harmony in relationships, being too accommodating means that others will not know how to help you when you need it, because they've never (or rarely) had to do so. Asking for help will throw them off, they won't know what to do, and you are unlikely to get what you need.

❀ ❀ ❀

Assumption: Don't be antisocial. People will think you don't like them if you'd rather spend time alone instead of with them.

Right: You have a right to be alone even if others would prefer your company.

Discussion: Some people might be offended that you would rather spend time alone than with them. Even so, be honest about your need for alone time when you need it or want it. It will make you more available to your friends and family when you are with them.

❀ ❀ ❀

Assumption: You should always have a good reason for what you feel and do. And you should be able to explain your reason to others' satisfaction. If you can't, then it isn't a good enough reason and you shouldn't feel that way.

Right: You have a right not to have to justify yourself to others.

Discussion: I've met plenty of people who believe this to be true and demand their partners explain themselves to their satisfaction. If the explanation isn't satisfactory to the first person, then they take the position that their partner has no right to feel that way. However, this position is optimally designed to justify the first person's perspective. If they decide the partner's position isn't supported well enough, then they may decide their partner's feelings aren't valid and won't feel the need to accommodate the partner.

❀ ❀ ❀

Assumption: When someone is in trouble, you should help them.

Right: You have a right not to be responsible for other people's behaviors, actions, feelings, or problems.

Discussion: This one needs to be balanced with what kind of help you can provide and whether your help will diminish your ability to meet your other responsibilities. Helping others is good, but not at your own expense.

❀ ❀ ❀

Assumption: You should be sensitive to the needs and wishes of others even when they are unable to tell you what they want.

Right: You have a right not to anticipate others' needs and wishes.

Discussion: Unless an adult is developmentally or cognitively impaired, they are capable of expressing their needs and wishes. While it feels good when someone "knows" what we like or need, this should be thought of as a bonus, not an expectation. Any adult who expects their partner to intuit what they need is acting like an infant who can only engage in protest behavior (i.e., crying) to get the parent's attention.

❀ ❀ ❀

Assumption: It's not nice to put people off. If someone asks you a question, give an answer.

<u>Right</u>: You have a right to choose not to respond to a situation.

<u>Discussion</u>: Some questions are not immediately answerable; it can take time to formulate an answer. In this case, it's okay to put people off. It is also okay to choose to maintain your privacy if you would prefer not to share.

❋ ❋ ❋

<u>Assumption</u>: If someone wrongs you, you should forgive them. It's the right thing to do.

<u>Right</u>: You have a right to decide when and whether to forgive someone else.

<u>Discussion</u>: While forgiveness is generally a good thing, it is only good if it is true forgiveness. Many of us were taught to forgive and forget. This isn't true forgiveness, but rather suppression of feelings and experience. Genuine forgiveness takes time—it doesn't come easily.

❋ ❋ ❋

If people find themselves in abusive relationships, they often make the assumption that that's what they deserve. In the process they give up a host of other rights in order to accommodate the relationship. There are resources for learning more about abusive relationships in the appendix.

There are several rights that may seem obvious but that are infringed upon in abusive relationships. Some of these rights include:

- A right to be in a non-abusive relationship
- A right to be safe.
- A right to love and to be loved.
- A right to dignity and respect.
- A right to privacy.
- A right to be uniquely your own person.
- A right to earn and control your own money.
- A right to relationships with friends and family.

While communicating assertively has some rules, which I will get to shortly, its most important principle is to believe that you have all the rights stated above, as does your partner. If you believe you and your partner both have these rights, then communicating assertively is a lot easier.

Six Guidelines for Effective Assertive Communication

Now let's take these rights and start communicating from an assertive position. As you learn to communicate more effectively, there are six guidelines to follow:

1. Be honest and open about how you feel. This requires you to be vulnerable—a scary proposition if you haven't done so before. Remember that be-

ing vulnerable is how people connect, and that's what you need—you need your partner to connect with you so you can tell the truth.

2. Focus on what you want, not on what your partner did. This is a hard one because it's easier to focus on what went wrong than on what we want. The trick is to ask yourself how you want to feel or what you want to have happen, not focus on how your partner is behaving. You want to get your point across to your partner—not point your finger.

3. Be specific about what you want. If you are general (e.g., "I need you to take more initiative around the house"), your partner has lots of room to get it wrong. Instead, be specific: "I want you to clean the kitchen after I cook dinner."

4. Have the conversation when you are calm so you can be matter-of-fact. This keeps your partner's defenses down. Getting to a state of calm about a situation that has upset you may require that you wait until the next day to talk about it. Sleep is good for helping us hit the reset button emotionally.

5. Avoid statements that are judgmental or that blame your partner. If you get judgy, your partner will get defensive and won't be able to listen to what you are saying—the opposite of communicating effectively.

6. Don't apologize for your wants or needs. Your desires are nothing to apologize for. If you want something from your partner, ask for it. He may push back or try to negotiate with you, and that's okay. But resist the urge to apologize.

When to Have the Conversation

One conundrum my clients find themselves in is trying to find the perfect time to have a difficult conversation. When they have something serious to discuss and they expect the topic to cause a conflict, they don't want to turn a nice time into a fight. On the other hand, they know that when they're already in a conflict with their partner, that's not a good time either. So, if they can't bring it up when their relationship is calm and happy and they can't bring it up when times are a little more difficult, when can they bring it up?

Because telling the truth sooner rather than later is important for your health and well-being as well as the health of your relationship, the time to bring something up is as close to the moment of realization of the truth as possible. That being said, being mindful of the state of your partner and the dynamic between the two of you is important, too. The best time to talk about a difficult topic is when the two of you are prepared to talk and are emotionally resilient. Being emotionally resilient is being able to keep your emotions in check, take in what's happening, and be flexible. Being well rested, fed, and in a good mood gives you the best opportunity for emotional resilience.

It follows then that if your partner is tired, hungry, in a bad mood, or preoccupied, bringing up a potential point of contention may not be ideal. However, this may be the time that you most want to talk. I'd suggest talking to your partner about a time he'd be able to have a conversation with you. Better yet, discuss having "relationship board meetings." These are meetings where you agree to talk about mundane things like division of household chores as well as disagreements. Find a regular time to meet and put it on each of your calendars. Bring up the idea of having these meetings when you have no pressing issue, or he may push to know what you want to talk about. Without a pressing relationship issue, you can talk about whether and when to have the meeting with no hidden agenda.

How to Have the Conversation

Here's where we put everything together and get to the nitty-gritty of the mechanics of assertive communication. To start with, I give my clients a three-part formula to follow:

1. Address the situation from your partner's perspective
2. Talk about how you are feeling and/or affected by the situation
3. Make a request

Gloria

Gloria plopped down on my couch and burst into tears. She and her husband had had another argument and she didn't know what to do. Through her tears she described what happened. For the last few months, Tony had been occupying his time in their garage with his projects, leaving Gloria with most of the responsibility for managing their two children and the household, as well as working her part-time job. She felt abandoned by him and no amount of asking him to help had changed this dynamic. She was at her wits' end. The most recent argument was after she asked him again to help her.

In many cases, when one partner has repeatedly asked the other for something to no avail, it is easy to get discouraged and quit asking. It can make someone feel like they don't deserve what they're asking for or that their partner doesn't really love them. If this has happened to you, consider changing your approach, not your message. If your message is your truth, then you need to stand by your truth. There are many ways to get your truth out there. Communicating assertively may help you be heard more easily.

Gloria acknowledged that she had stormed into the garage and demanded, "What is so important out here that you are ignoring your family?" She understood that wasn't the best approach, but she was hurt and frustrated. She felt she had been quite clear with Tony over the past several weeks and she was losing her patience.

Using this information and the three-part strategy for assertive communication, we constructed a way for Gloria to approach Tony and tell him what she needed. We started by taking a look at what was happening from Tony's perspective. Gloria told me that he was working more than fifty hours a week on a project at work. She imagined that he was physically tired at the end of the day and feeling stressed from work pressures. He probably felt like he needed to relax, but found their young children noisy and stressful. She knew he didn't like doing chores, but she didn't understand why he didn't want to talk with her about his stress. She understood more after I explained that talking about something stressful often just amplifies the stress.

What Gloria most needed Tony to understand is that she was in a similar situation and she needed his support. She managed the children, cleaned the house, and worked at least twenty hours a week. She often felt stressed and would feel better if she felt connected with Tony. She felt connected with Tony when they talked and when they worked together on something like making dinner, managing the children, or doing chores. Although she also felt connected when they talked, she realized that she didn't always want to talk about her problems either.

Gloria began to realize that because Tony was spending all his time in the garage, she was feeling alone and disconnected. She wondered whether he still loved her or if he was having an affair.

Let's put this information together and see what Gloria could say to Tony using this communication technique.

We will start with Gloria talking to Tony about the situation from his perspective:

> *Honey, I know you've been working hard and there is a lot of pressure at work to get this project done. I can imagine that at the end of the day you are tired and just want to relax. I know that kids aren't always the most relaxing people to be around and doing chores isn't pleasant either.*

Then we move on to how the situation is affecting Gloria:

> *When I'm left alone to manage the children and do the household chores, I feel alone and disconnected from you. Sometimes I even wonder if you are having an affair, and that makes me feel anxious. That's when I get upset with you like I did last week.*

Finally, Gloria could make a clear and specific request of Tony:

> *I'd like to talk about how I can get the help I need from you and you can get the relaxation you need.*

If we go back to the six guidelines to see how Gloria constructed a way to tell Tony what she wanted from him without blaming him, we see that she was honest and specific, she focused on what she wanted (not on what he did), she was calm, she didn't apologize, and she didn't blame him. She used the three-part strategy to create a script. The script helped her remain focused and calm and kept her from blaming him. Notice she was also mindful that Tony probably had needs of his own, so rather than placing a demand on him, she requested they talk about how each of them could get their individual needs met.

Now it's your turn. Go to the Worksheet for Communicating Effectively in the appendix to work on how to talk assertively to your partner about something that is upsetting you.

Rule Recap

Rule #1: Tell the Truth Sooner Rather than Later

Telling the truth keeps your integrity intact. Telling the truth sooner rather than later keeps you from experiencing the higher cost of allowing a lie to be believed for a longer period of time.

Three Ways to Lie

- Bald-faced lie
- Lie of omission
- Lie by diversion from the truth

Why People Lie

- To protect themselves
- To promote themselves
- To impact others
- Unknown reasons

Six Guidelines of Effective Communication

1. Be open and honest with how you feel.
2. Focus on what you want, NOT on what you don't want.
3. Be specific.
4. Have the conversation when you are calm.
5. Avoid judgmental and blaming statements.
6. Don't apologize for your wants or needs.

Assertive Communication Strategy

1. Address the situation from your partner's perspective
2. Talk about how you are feeling and/or affected by the situation
3. Make a request

Tips

- Have conversations when both parties are prepared to talk and are emotionally resilient.
- Avoid talking when you are tired, hungry, stressed, or preoccupied.
- Consider having relationship board meetings on a regular basis to talk about both mundane issues and disagreements.

Rule #2:
When Someone
Shows You Who
They Are,
Believe Them

There is a message in the way someone treats you. Just listen . . .

~r.h. Sin

Actions vs. Words

ONE OF THE BEST quotes about being in relationships and telling the truth I've seen is from Maya Angelou: "When someone shows you who they are, believe them." I think the most important word in this quote is "show." What people show you is more important than what they say about themselves. All people are blind to some degree as to how they come across. Anyone can tell you how kind and compassionate they are, but observe their behavior and see whether they act as kind and compassionate as they say they are.

Just as I discussed with the first rule, it can be hard to tell the truth to others, but it's equally hard—if not harder—to tell the truth to ourselves. Especially when the stakes are high. This rule is going to explore the saying "Actions speak louder than words." Paying attention to what you experience when another person's actions are hurtful, unreliable, untrustworthy, etc., is a form of telling yourself the truth. It's a truth that is hard to hear when you are married to or have fallen for someone who is not treating you well.

There are several ways people can and will show you who they are, but if you are not used to looking for them, they can be quite difficult to see. If you prefer to listen to what people say about themselves and have a hard time understanding why they behave the way they do, you are prone to being deceived. People will explain away or cover up their behavior, either intentionally or not.

Adam and Nora

Adam was repairing some dry rot around a window when he needed more nails at the hardware store. Because he didn't want to stop what he was doing, he asked Nora to go buy them. She was in the middle of her own project and told him she could go later, but wasn't available right now. Adam, who was already frustrated with the project, complained angrily that she was being self-ish.

If Nora only listened to Adam's words, she could come away from the interaction believing that she was being selfish. But if she stops and looks at Adam's outburst and what his behavior is showing her, she would realize that her response to Adam's request was reasonable and he was being selfish by trying to manipulate her into complying with his request.

Adam didn't know that he was projecting his own selfishness onto Nora. If Nora hadn't been paying attention, she wouldn't have realized that he was framing her experience to suit his own needs. The drive to look good to our partners and better than our behavior suggests is a strong one; people often aren't aware they are doing it. Adam was doing it and Nora needed to be able to see it was happening or she might blame herself for not helping him with his project.

Red Flags

When people first meet up and start seeing each other, there is often a period of time when one or both start wondering if the negative things they are seeing in the other person are one-off events or red flags. Red flags are difficult to see at the beginning of a relationship because we don't have enough data. However, here is something to consider: If someone misbehaves early on in the relationship, that same behavior is likely to be worse later on. In the beginning, we are all on our best behavior. If red flags emerge early when someone is on their best behavior, you should question how much worse it could get, not whether you should excuse it.

Aisha and Charles

Aisha is the executive director of a large nonprofit and is frequently involved in fundraising events for her organization as well as others. She has been single for the last few years, but recently met a man she really likes. She had been dating Charles for a few weeks when she invited him to a fundraiser. She was excited to introduce him to some of her friends and enjoy an evening of good food and entertainment with him. Everything went well until the end of the evening; Charles had too much to drink and they ended up arguing about whether he should take a cab home.

At our next coaching session, Aisha worried about what this meant. She had seen Charles have a cocktail or glass of wine with dinner, but didn't think that much about it. Now she wondered whether he had a drinking problem. What she didn't know was whether getting drunk was an inadvertent, one-time situation or a regular occurrence.

One of the factors clouding her judgment was her knowledge that Charles had been going through a particularly rough time with his ex-wife over custody arrangements for their two children. She reasoned that his stress level could have contributed to him drinking too much on this occasion, but that drinking too much was not generally a problem for him.

If Aisha followed Maya Angelou's advice, she would have made the assumption that Charles had a drinking problem. After all, in this one instance he had shown her a side of himself that suggested a problem. First, he conducted himself poorly early on in the relationship. Then, not only did he not know when to stop drinking, but he was also unable to listen to Aisha when she suggested he take a cab home. However, Aisha wasn't quite ready to assume his drinking was a problem and end the relationship; she wanted to give him the benefit of the doubt. She and Charles came to an understanding of how his behavior affected her and they continued dating for several more months.

Of course no one is perfect and we all struggle with problems. The question is how to know whether a problem is more than a relationship can or should bear. When should we give someone the benefit of the doubt? When should we cut our losses and move on? The answers depend on a lot of factors, and each person has to weigh the options carefully.

So what happened with Aisha and Charles? After several more months of dating, it became clear to Aisha that the problem behaviors present during that drunken evening were just a glimpse into larger issues Charles had with drinking and listening to his partner. In the end she broke off the relationship. In hindsight she said she should have broken it off after the fundraiser, because it would have been easier at that point.

In marriages, red flags are a different issue. Dating relationships are far easier to end than marriages are. As we will see in the next story, red flags in marriages show up as changes in behavior or routines that could be explained more than one way. How you choose to explain those changes to yourself will dictate what choices you make about the relationship.

Confirmation Bias

We humans frequently make an unfortunate error when we interpret the meaning of something: the error of confirmation bias, or the phenomenon of seeing what we expect to see. Our brains have a tendency to interpret ambiguous information in ways that support our beliefs and expectations. Although this bias is so subtle we often don't realize we're falling prey to it, it can have devastating consequences.

Josh and Mika

Even though they had only been dating a month, Josh was constantly checking in with Mika. He wanted to know where she was and who she was with at all times. Mika found this endearing because she thought it meant Josh loved her. Unfortunately, this kind of behavior isn't love; it's jealousy and possession, which are toxic ingredients in relationships. Mika's misinterpretation of Josh's behavior caused her enormous problems when he showed up at her work and accused her of cheating on him, causing a scene and embarrassing Mika in front of her co-workers.

While this is a dramatic example, this kind of thing happens all the time in more insidious ways within relationships. We expect things to be one way and we don't want to know or can't tolerate them being another way; we don't want to know the truth. We don't want to believe our partner would lie, cheat, or steal. We want to believe he is honest and trustworthy. If your partner is doing something and covering it up, you may ignore the warning signs because you simply don't want to know the truth. It's one thing to do this if your partner is planning a surprise party for you, but another thing entirely if he is engaged in an activity that is harmful to you.

Raylene and Gary

Raylene and Gary had been married for nearly ten years. She worked full-time at a job she enjoyed, but Gary had been unemployed for the last year. As a result of being unable to find work and provide for their family (they had three children and two dogs), Gary was depressed and becoming increasingly desperate. One day while running errands, he ran into an old high school buddy who told him about making money by trading old and rare coins. Gary knew that he and Raylene didn't have the money to start a business like that, but he reasoned that if he got started by using a credit card he could get a profitable business going and pay off the debt before Raylene found out. He thought this would be an easy way to generate income and contribute meaningfully to the family. Although Raylene might be upset at first, she'd be glad he figured out a way to make money.

Gary applied for a new credit card and began buying coins. Finding and buying coins took up the majority of his time. He stored his growing collection in the garage, which would keep Raylene from seeing it since she rarely went in there. He started picking up the mail and paying the bills so she wouldn't know about the new credit card. One day a delivery of coins arrived at the house while Raylene was home. When she asked Gary what he had purchased, he lied to her, saying it was an old set of plates for his mother's birthday that he found at a thrift store. He took the package to the garage and hoped Raylene would forget about it.

There were several signs that Raylene didn't pick up on. She had no reason to go into the garage, didn't know about the new credit card, and thought Gary was taking initiative and responsibility when he started paying the bills. It didn't occur to her that thrift stores don't deliver packages. Although she was irritated with Gary for neglecting many of the household chores he had been doing until recently, she excused him because he said he was job hunting and he had started paying the bills, which she despised doing. She believed him and didn't follow up when he gave vague answers about possible jobs and failed to fill her in on job interviews. She knew he'd been struggling with depression and she didn't want to make him feel worse by bringing up the job search if it wasn't going well. Again and again, she failed to follow up on odd behavior, strange occurrences, and vague answers.

Raylene believed Gary had the family's best interest at heart; she failed to understand the meaning of the changes in his routine. She knew he had a history of a gambling problem, but it had been over eight years since that was a problem; she had long ago stopped worrying about it. She later told me that if she'd thought about the changes and Gary's history of gambling, she would have questioned him more and gone into the garage sooner. Raylene had succumbed to confirmation bias despite what she knew about Gary. He had shown her early in their marriage that he had an addiction that made him susceptible to poor decision-making, especially during times of stress.

Let's take a step back here and clarify that I'm not blaming Raylene for what was happening. She was blind-sided by Gary's duplicity, and it was not her fault. I'm using this story as an example of confirmation bias at work in a way that often shows up in relationships. This story illustrates how a belief or expectation can color your interpretation of another person's behavior and the ease with which we can excuse behavior in our partners. In this case, Raylene was interpreting Gary's new behavior in a way that made it support her expectation that he was reliable and working in the best interest of the family. Her interpretation was easy to make because this is how marriages are "supposed" to work. You are supposed to be able to rely on and trust your partner.

Let's continue the story.

One day Raylene came home early and, knowing Gary was home, started looking for him. What she found when she made her way to the garage was almost beyond her ability to comprehend. There were five or six display cases stacked with boxes of coins and books on collecting coins. Gary was at a desk intently inspecting a coin through a magnifying glass. He didn't hear her come into the garage.

Raylene was so taken aback that she didn't know what to make of it. She had no idea what was going on or what it meant. It didn't take her long to realize that Gary had been deceiving her. She confronted him, and he couldn't hide what had been going on. Although he knew that he had kept this scheme from her, he thought she'd be okay with his efforts to put something into place to bring in income. He expected her to be upset with him, but thought that ultimately she would be happy with his initiative and creativity.

Once Raylene learned what Gary had been doing and about his deception, she had a decision to make. She and I talked at length about her options. As she saw it she could either support him in his venture or leave him. They had been married for ten years and ending the marriage would have devastating consequences for them, their financial situation, and their children. She and the children would be unable to afford to live in the house, a divorce would be very disruptive to the children, and she didn't want to think of the financial burden this would place on everyone.

On the other hand, Raylene realized that Gary's incredible lack of respect for her and their marriage was no small matter. It wasn't just that, however; he had also destroyed their credit by substantially increasing their debt and failing to pay several bills. Gary had showed that he was irresponsible and deceptive and Raylene felt she could no longer count on him as an emotional or financial partner.

To hear Gary talk about what he had done, you might think that he was a good guy trying to provide for his family, but his behavior demonstrated something quite different. If Raylene listened to what he said, she would have bought into his scheme and supported him. Instead, she looked at what his behavior was showing her. She didn't try to gloss over what happened; she stared directly into the truth of the situation and responded accordingly. She took the children and left.

This story illustrates in a dramatic fashion how confirmation bias works. It might be hard to imagine how something like this could play out in your marriage. Let's look at a different story, one that is a little subtler and I've seen more than once in relationships.

Aaron and Dana

Aaron was often irritable with his wife, Dana, because she didn't do things the way he liked them to be done. When he was particularly irritated with her, he didn't hesitate to tell her what she was doing wrong. He was always careful to explain to her that he had her best interest in mind when he corrected her. After all, if she would just change her behavior, she'd be more efficient and effective and people would like her more; he wants the best for her. Unfortunately, his constant corrections had a negative effect on Dana. She felt insecure and like a real screw-up. She didn't get angry with Aaron, though, because she believed him when he said he had her best interest in mind.

How would you feel if Dana was your friend and you saw Aaron treating her like that? His behavior suggests he believes he knows better than she does. If he had her best interest at heart he would be acknowledging her strengths, not picking on her. He would have her back; he wouldn't constantly try to fix her. This is a great example of confirmation bias: Dana wants to believe that her life partner has her best interest at heart, so when he criticizes her she uses the criticism to confirm her belief.

These stories are good examples of how confirmation bias shows up in our relationships. We accept our partner's projections of their negative emotional reactions, we excuse red flags, and we believe our partner's version of what just happened. How are you supposed to overcome confirmation bias? How do you know if what you are seeing can be taken at face value or if you need to assume the worst?

Overcoming Confirmation Bias

It's not a pleasant idea that you might not be able to trust your partner. I get it. Plus, your partner isn't perfect, and expecting perfection is no way to conduct a healthy relationship. On the other hand, you don't want to be blindsided. It's better to learn and understand the truth of a difficult situation earlier than to let it go on for too long.

Strive for a balance: Trust your partner, but pay attention to odd behavior. One or two odd changes are probably not a big deal, but if there is a string of changes or odd behavior, there's something to explore. It may mean nothing, so don't jump to conclusions. There are four steps to keeping an open mind without becoming distrustful or paranoid.

- Pay attention to your unease
- Be open to alternative explanations (not just your default)
- Talk to a friend
- Pay attention to future behavior

Pay Attention to Your Unease

This is important because your subconscious mind will often pick up on something being off before you become fully aware of it. If you notice an unease, at least make note of it.

What do I mean by unease? I mean that feeling you have when you notice something and it strikes you as odd or you ask yourself what that was about. If you find yourself quickly following up a feeling of unease with a plausible reason that makes you feel better, you may be right or you may be falling prey to confirmation bias. The best thing to do is to notice what happened and how it made you feel. Check in to see whether you've had similar feelings of unease recently. If not, you're probably right; it's nothing to be concerned about. If you have had similar feelings, though, start paying better attention and asking more questions.

If your partner comes home smelling like another woman's perfume, ask him about it. He'll probably say a co-worker gave him a hug for some reason. It makes you feel uncomfortable just a little. You don't like that he hugged another woman, but you don't think he'd have an affair. It might be just what he says. You won't know any differently unless you pay attention. It's not time yet to jump to conclusions; just make a note and pay attention to whether other evidence pops up and he starts coming home late, going out without you, not answering his phone during the day, etc. Any one of these behaviors might not mean anything, but if you start putting them together, a different picture emerges. If you don't make note of these moments of unease as they pop up but instead explain them away, you won't have them to refer to later.

Be Open to Alternative Explanations

You want to know the truth and to tell yourself the truth sooner rather than later. The sooner you know a problematic truth, the easier it is to address the problem. If you are listening to any unease that shows up, you can generate other explanations for what you noticed. Your husband says a co-worker gave him a hug. That may be true and innocent enough. What other explanations could there be? He hugged a co-worker, but it isn't innocent. It wasn't a co-worker he hugged, but someone else. Maybe that someone else is your friend and he hugged her because they got together and are planning a surprise for you. That's an innocent enough explanation. What's important is not jumping to conclusions or making any assumptions. Be open to alternative explanations, even when some of the alternatives are unpleasant to think about.

Talk to a Friend

It is difficult to avoid succumbing to confirmation bias, making assumptions, and jumping to conclusions. This is where a trusted friend can come in handy. Get your friend on board with the importance of not jumping to conclusions about what is happening. Sometimes our friends, in an effort to be on our side, will get dramatic and inflame the situation rather than taking a neutral supportive stance. If you don't have such a friend, talk to a coach or therapist.

Explain what you saw and ask your friend to help you come up with possible explanations. Then keep these explanations in mind. If further odd behaviors or vague explanations make you feel unease, see which alternative explanations still fit with what is happening.

Pay Attention to Future Behavior

The goal here is to see if there is indeed a string of behavior, and if so, which of your alternative explanations fits what you're seeing. I included this step because it is easy to forget about the past. If you attribute an odd occurrence or two to something benign and forget about it, then you are more likely to miss a pattern. Keep talking with your friend. Even if you feel you can eliminate one or more explanations, be careful. If you start feeling alarmed, you are likely to focus on one explanation and start making assumptions. If you continue to encounter that feeling of unease, check out what's happening with your partner. I'd suggest referring to the section on communicating effectively for tips on how to have the conversation. State what you are noticing, how it makes you feel, and ask for an explanation.

The Flipside

The point of Rule #2 is to pay attention to what your partner is doing and how he is behaving. His behavior will tell you a lot about him and his values. While the stories I've provided up to this point highlight undesirable behaviors, this isn't the entire picture. While it's easy to get caught up in the grind of day-to-day life and fail to notice changes in behavior or decisions your partner makes that may have devastating consequences for you or the relationship, it is also just as easy, if not easier, to fail to notice his good qualities.

Noticing and acknowledging what your partner is doing well is one of the most important things you can do to foster the health of your relationship. I often hear from disgruntled women complaining about their spouses. These men can't seem to get anything right and their wives let no opportunity go by to tell them how disappointed or angry they are with their behavior. It could be as insidious as not doing anything around the house unless asked, to not doing things the way she expects or when she expects them to be done. By the time I hear about how unhappy a woman is with her marriage, she's practically spitting nails.

One of the easiest ways to get your partner to help out around the house is to notice what he does and express appreciation for his help. People love to help and will often do so for the sheer pleasure of receiving acknowledgment.

Unfortunately we often expect that telling our partner what we want once should be sufficient to get them to change their behavior. After all, if they really loved us they would pay attention to what we want and avoid hurting our feelings and causing arguments. Not only that, most of what these disgruntled women complain about is basic consideration for others. It's not rocket science. Getting dirty clothes into the hamper, taking shoes off at the door, getting everything on the grocery list or putting things away in the proper place; none of these requests seem difficult. How hard can it be to load the dishwasher after dinner or make the bed in the morning without being asked? Is it really so hard to wash stubble down the drain after shaving?

You don't always know what's going on when your partner can't seem to do the simplest things and you find yourself becoming a nag. It could be stress, lack of attention to detail, disengagement from the relationship, or any number of other problems. However, one thing that's universal is the pleasure people receive from being acknowledged for their contributions and what they did well.

Whether you and your partner you are getting along or not, I'd suggest noticing when he shows you he means well and he's trying. Focus on what he does well and what he does right, and tell him that you noticed—even if what he did wasn't perfect.

Train Your Partner, Don't Nag

There is a principle of successive approximation at work here. That's jargon for getting closer and closer to what you want. It can be hard to achieve when you are upset with your spouse because you don't want to acknowledge halfhearted attempts at what seem like simple tasks.

Take putting dirty clothes in the hamper as an example. If your husband leaves his clothes wherever he happens to remove them, you'll have dirty laundry scattered from the back door to the bedroom. It seems a simple task to pick up clothes and put them in the hamper. Let's assume you've asked him to do so, but for some reason he always "forgets." You could nag him, but face it, nagging doesn't work and it makes you even more frustrated. You don't like how nagging makes you feel, and it certainly doesn't make him feel good.

Using successive approximation, tell him you appreciate him leaving his jeans and socks in the bedroom (near the hamper) because it makes your life easier. Ignore all the other articles of clothing that were left in other areas of the house. Later, when some of his clothes actually make it into the hamper, acknowledge it and thank him for making your life easier by getting clothes into the hamper. This time, ignore all instances when his clothes did not make it into the hamper, even if they made it into the bedroom. If you keep doing this, over time more and more of his clothes will make it into the hamper. He will work for the acknowledgment that he did something you like. (By the way, this works for children, too.) Essentially, your acknowledgment and praise will reinforce behavior that is closer and closer to the behavior you want.

If you take a step back and think about this for a moment, it makes a certain amount of sense. If you pay positive attention to what you want or like in someone, they will give you more of that. If your attention is negative and critical, they will pull away from you. You've probably heard the research that good relationships have a favorable ratio of positive statements to negative statements. Usually the ratio reported in the research is in the neighborhood of five to one: five positive statements for every negative statement. If you resort to nagging your husband to get him to do what you want, that's a lot of negative statements to make up for!

Rule Recap

Rule #2: When Someone Shows You Who They Are, Believe Them

People will tell you they are better people than they actually are. In the beginning of a relationship, you don't have enough information to know any better, but actions speak louder than words. Pay attention to what people do more than what they say.

Confirmation bias is the tendency to take ambiguous information and create an explanation that fits current beliefs and expectations. People unknowingly use confirmation bias to explain red flags.

Red flags are behaviors you notice but don't know what to do with. Is the red flag something to pay attention to or should you give the benefit of the doubt? People are on their best behavior at the beginning of a relationship, so red flags that appear then should be given more weight, not the benefit of the doubt. Once you see a red flag, look for other behaviors that confirm the problem it signals.

Red flags in marriages are changes in behavior patterns and are usually (at least initially) easy to explain away—confirmation bias again.

Avoid falling prey to confirmation bias using these four steps:
1. Pay attention to your unease.
2. Generate alternative explanations.
3. Talk with a friend or coach.
4. Watch future behavior.

Notice positive behaviors, too. Use the principle of successive approximation to notice changes for the better, even if they are not perfect. People of all ages respond to praise.

Rule #3:
Always Assume
the Best in Your
Partner

Through judging, we separate.
Through understanding, we grow.

~Doe Zantamata

How Negative Assumptions Corrode Your Relationship

AFTER YEARS OF WORKING with individuals and hearing them complain about their spouses, I've noticed a particularly insidious pattern. Let's say I'm seeing a woman who is angry with her husband for various and repeated infractions over the years. At some point she started believing that he was purposefully doing things to hurt and upset her. Most of the time, people in this situation don't remember when this assumption started, but by the time they start working with me, it's been happening for quite a while.

There is some logic to this assumption. After years of living with someone, you know what upsets them. That makes it seem reasonable to assume your partner makes decisions he knows will hurt or upset you. But that logic is an emotional logic. It assumes that your partner wants you to be hurt, which is highly unlikely.

Making this kind of assumption is hurtful to the relationship. True, you are in a position to make an assumption like this because you are feeling hurt, but doing so only compounds the problem. Your brain is relying on information from an often painful past to fill in the gaps, so when you make an assumption you are essentially stuck in the past. Since our brains are always alert to possible threats and painful situations, if it is remotely possible for your brain to fill in the information gap and assume you will be hurt, it will. This is how it protects you from the possibility of being hurt. Better safe than sorry, right?

Wrong! Because if you rely on your assumptions, you are essentially failing to find out what you don't know. You are being lazy and not taking responsibility for your present and future selves. The more you rely on your assumptions, the more you will lash out at others, remain in a negative mindset, and stew in your pain and misery.

You have control over how you interpret your partner's behavior. Do you assume he doesn't know what he's doing? That he doesn't pay attention? That he's communicating his disregard for you? That he intends to upset you? These are all dangerous assumptions.

The problem here is that when we make assumptions, we often don't realize we've done so. We think we have some authentic window into the nature of reality. We think we know something that we do not in fact know. Assumptions are a naturally occurring function of the brain. There is a blind spot on your retina that has no light receptors. Your brain makes an assumption about what is there, but when the eye doctor has you stare at a dot and push a button when you see lights flashing around you, there's an area in your visual field where you can't see the flashing light. Your brain doesn't know there is a flashing light because it cannot see the light, and because it can't see the light, it doesn't fill in the gap with a flashing light. Your brain's assumptions about your blind spot are inaccurate.

A similar phenomenon happens with memory. Your memory consists of a few snippets of an event. When you recall the event, you recall the snippets and fill in the gaps. That's why the more often you retell a memory the more distorted the memory becomes. Your recollection of the gaps changes, so the specific details are easy to get wrong. Think of those stories of fishermen whose fish get bigger every time they retell the story. Or the study that shows if you're asked how fast the car was going when it smashed into the pole you'll estimate a higher speed than if you're asked how fast it was going when it bumped into the pole. You witnessed the car hitting the pole, but specifically how fast the car was going is not in your memory. You have to make a guess, and you guess wrong because of the word used to describe the event.

Making assumptions and filling in gaps in information is part of how your brain naturally functions. Unfortunately, this can trip you up in major ways, especially when you blindly or automatically make assumptions about another person's intent or about the future. If your assumption is automatic (not something you gave much thought to), you should assume it's wrong. The likelihood that you are right is so low that you'd be better off assuming you are wrong. That way you'll at least be right about something!

Taylor and Brad

Taylor and Brad have three young children. At the end of her work day, Taylor picks the children up from daycare. By the time she gets home, Brad is making dinner. They live in a townhouse with one parking space near their front door and they rent another space about a block away. Taylor has asked Brad to park in the rented space so she has an easier time getting the children out of the car and into the house at the end of the day. However, several times a week, Brad parks in the space near the front door and forgets to move his car. It has gotten to the point that when he parks in the space near the door and she has to park in the rented space, she feels angry and resentful. It doesn't feel like he respects how hard she works and how difficult it is to manage three children at the end of the day. This isn't the only issue like this in their marriage. Incidents like this have caused Taylor to assume that Brad doesn't care about her, doesn't respect how hard she works, and may even be doing this just to make her work harder.

Taylor and Brad have had several discussions about where to park and Taylor has good reasons for parking near the front door. Because she feels she has been clear and Brad expresses understanding and agreement in their discussions, when Brad parks in the space near the front door, Taylor is left wondering why he's doing this.

There is ambiguity here, and this is where assumptions come into play. In order to reduce the ambiguity, Taylor starts looking for answers to her question. When she finds an answer that seems to make sense, she will feel like the question has been answered. Thus an automatic assumption will be born.

What was ambiguous about this situation? The reason Brad is parking near the front door despite repeated requests to leave the space for Taylor. Possible reasons might be that Brad is being thoughtless, that he doesn't really care how hard Taylor is working, that he doesn't take her seriously, that he got distracted, that he has poor follow-through and is not reliable, that he forgot, etc.

It was easy for Taylor to be charitable in her interpretations the first time or two it happened. She reasoned that Brad must have been in a hurry and forgot to move the car. Another time she thought he must have been distracted when he drove up. However, after the tenth time, she wasn't feeling as charitable. She started feeling like her charitable assumptions and Brad's explanations weren't the truth. If they were, he wouldn't keep doing it. Brad's repeated offenses become part of the ambiguity.

Because Taylor doesn't know or understand why this is happening and because she is having an intense negative emotional reaction, the answer she selects will most likely be consistent with how she feels. Shortly after she and Brad talked about the situation and reached an agreement, she felt understood and respected. The first couple of times he parked in the space near the door, because she felt good about their agreement, her annoyance didn't affect her interpretation. However by the tenth time, she felt disrespected and neglected, so the explanation that felt right is that he didn't either take her seriously or he didn't care about her.

Make Deliberate Assumptions Instead

Your brain naturally makes assumptions. In some sense, there is nothing you can do about it. However, it is possible to use it to your benefit. You just need to be intentional about the process.

If you assume the best of your partner, you hold him to a higher standard. You leave the responsibility for his behavior with him and allow him to experience the consequences if he gets it wrong. When you assume the best and your partner doesn't do his best, his failure is more obvious. Although he could get defensive about getting it wrong, he can't get defensive about you accusing, blaming, or nagging him, because you didn't do those things.

If you assume the worst and point it out to him by accusing, blaming, or nagging, he is likely to focus on your behavior and not take responsibility for his behavior.

Here is how this works. To start, recognize when you are making assumptions in an attempt to make sense of a situation. There are things you don't know or understand and assumptions help bring down your feelings of ambiguity. However, no matter how right the assumption feels, the likelihood of it being right is low, regardless of how well you know your partner.

Since the act of making an assumption is essentially an act of making up a story to justify how you feel, you are free to assume whatever you want. You can deliberately make an assumption that creates a positive story. It won't be any more true than the negative assumption would be, so you may as well.

Our partners often give us plenty of reasons to make negative assumptions about them. I know plenty of women who don't believe their partners are capable of taking care of the kids, cleaning the house, getting to appointments on time, or doing the grocery shopping. Their partners have different priorities, different timelines, and don't do things the way they want them done. These differences are upsetting to women whose lives are a finely tuned choreography of working, parenting, maintaining the house, having friends, and being married. The demands feel endless and women often feel like they are barely keeping up. It feels as if tasks and errands need to be done a specific way or the whole system will come crashing down.

Although it may feel this way, it isn't that bad. Make the assumption that your partner can handle it. As long as he isn't putting anyone's life at risk, see what happens. He may not get things done on your time frame or in the exact manner you'd like them done, but if he gets them done, how much does it really matter that they aren't exactly to your preference? Take a breath, let it go, and thank him for his efforts.

Reversing Anger with Empathy

Unfortunately, many women who don't feel supported by their partners end up with chronic anger over their partner's lack of participation. This makes it incredibly difficult to assume the best. In this case, at a minimum acknowledge that you are missing information. Take a step back and don't fill in the gap. By not making an assumption, you'll stay open to possibilities and make it easier to keep your anger manageable. Ask your partner questions to clarify the missing information instead of launching into how upset you are. You never know; you may learn something. It may not be what you expect to learn, but staying open to the possibility may surprise you.

If you feel your partner is doing things to intentionally upset or ignore you, you probably repeatedly feel like your partner doesn't understand you and doesn't understand how hurtful he's being. If he did, he wouldn't be that way. If he really loved you, he'd pay more attention and make more of an effort. You reason he must lack empathy for you and your situation and care only about himself. It's only natural to be defensive and angry with him in this case, but your anger pulls you out of an empathic state. At this point, neither one of you is being empathic and you are both likely making assumptions about the other. Essentially, this is a pattern of the two of you being out of touch with each other, foregoing empathy, making assumptions, and expecting the other to change.

If you are in the habit of assuming he's intentionally out to upset or ignore you, it won't take much to make you angry with him. Stopping these types of assumptions will go a long way in improving the tone of your relationship. It will reduce your resentment and make it easier to resolve issues. I'm not promising it will cure all the problems in your marriage, but changing this one pattern will help your relationship.

In Taylor's situation, once she took a step back and realized she was making an automatic assumption that Brad didn't take her seriously, she realized that she had lots of evidence to the contrary. That meant her assumption couldn't be true and there had to be a better explanation. Although they had talked about where to park on several occasions, talking about it obviously wasn't the solution to the problem. Taylor began texting Brad to let him know she was leaving the daycare and would be home in about ten minutes. She reasoned that should give him plenty of time to move the car if necessary. This new strategy worked about 90% of the time and reduced her frustration with him. After further exploration of other problems in their relationship, Brad was diagnosed with Attention Deficit Hyperactivity Disorder (ADHD), which makes it difficult to track details. This explanation for Brad's behavior helped Taylor continue to question her automatic assumptions when she became angry with him and to make a more deliberate assumption that he was doing his best, even if it didn't look that way.

You Have to Be the One to Move First

Here is a hard truth, a truth my clients don't necessarily like to hear: If you recognize that something needs to change, you cannot demand he change before you do. No matter how hurt and angry you are and how much you need your partner to demonstrate that he cares, it's more important to change the dynamic than to demand he make the first move. If you persist with this demand, you will wait a long time, nothing will change, and you will continue to be unhappy.

Why do you have to be the one that makes the changes? Because you are the one struggling with the problem. While he is also hurt and angry, you are reading this book looking for answers. Therefore it is your responsibility to try what you're learning. Take responsibility for your own emotional state and process.

Calming your anger, especially if it is chronic, is a difficult task. It will take persistence and practice on your part. Just reducing the volume on your anger to a manageable level is a step in the right direction. Approach this exercise for your own sake, not for his or for the sake of the relationship. Instead, strive to be less controlled by feeling angry. Doing so is good for you and the rest of your family whether or not it improves your relationship.

Six Steps to Calming Your Anger

There are six steps to calming your anger so you can see the pattern and change your assumptions. Once you change your assumptions, the way you interact will naturally shift. The first three steps are good to practice on a regular basis when you are by yourself and have time to think. The last three steps are meant for interactions with your partner in real time.

1. Notice your feelings. There is a difference between feelings (in your body) and emotions (in your head). When we are trying to quell a negative emotional state, we are trying to get the bodily feeling to go away. We primarily want the feeling resolved, as opposed to the emotion. Rather than lashing out or apologizing inappropriately, try to tolerate the feeling so it doesn't overwhelm you. Try this breathing exercise: Focus on the unpleasant feeling in your body and take seven slow, deep breaths. At the end of the seven breaths, notice how the feeling has changed. It should have decreased. If not, repeat the exercise.

2. Set an intention. Decide how you want things to be different and set your intention for that change. Focus on what you'd like to have happen instead of

what the past has led you to expect. This step works best if you are focusing on a particular interaction, rather than a general state. If you have a request for your partner, what do you want your partner to say or do in response? If he responds this way, how will it make you feel? Focus on that feeling and think about your request from that state, rather than from an angry state.

3. Listen to your assumptions. As you set your intention, notice the things you are saying to yourself and the assumptions you are making. Do you hear yourself blaming him for how you feel? "He's such a jerk!" (Blaming statement.) "He doesn't care about how I feel." (Assumption.) When these thoughts come up, recognize what they are and change your focus back to how you want to feel and what you want from him.

Do these next three steps when you are in the middle of a conversation or argument with your partner. The first few times, do it during casual conversation for practice. It will be easier when you are calm.

4. Listen to your partner. An interesting phenomenon in relationships is that both parties typically want the same thing and feel the same when in the midst of a fight. Have you ever had a fight where both of you insisted the other wasn't listening? Guess what: You both felt misunderstood. When you feel misunderstood, you don't realize that your partner

feels the same way you do. There's a bit of irony! At the end of the day, everyone wants to feel understood, and the path to understanding is empathic listening. When a conflict arises, move into a listening mode. Seek to understand where he's coming from and what he wants by listening to him.

5. Identify how your partner is feeling. Imagine how you'd feel if the roles were reversed. Chances are good that's the way he feels. However, you don't know that to be true unless you ask, so the next step is . . .

6. Check in with your partner. How does he label his feelings? Does he feel understood by you? Ask something such as, "Are you [upset/angry/sad] because you wanted me to [fill in the blank]?" Even if you get it wrong, it's okay. He'll correct you and will likely feel better that you are striving to understand him.

When It's Not Enough

If he isn't changing his behavior despite your positive assumptions, encouragement, and use of effective communication, it's time to consider getting professional help. Either he or you could be experiencing something that needs more support, skill, and knowledge than either of you can bring to the relationship. Issues such as depression, life stressors, trauma, and attention deficit hyperactivity disorder are just a few of the problems that can affect one partner and jeopardize the relationship despite both partners' best efforts.

Rule Recap

Rule #3: Always Assume the Best in Your Partner

Assumptions are usually automatic and negative. While these kinds of assumptions are part of how your brain functions, they can be detrimental to a relationship. Automatic assumptions keep you stuck in the past and closed off to change for the better.

We make assumptions when there are gaps in what we know, when information is ambiguous. Recognize the ambiguity and seek to find the answers instead of making assumptions.

When you make an assumption, be deliberate about it. Since an assumption is a story you are telling yourself that fills in the gaps of your knowledge, tell yourself a positive story. You're making it up anyway, and you're likely to be wrong. You may as well be wrong in a happy way!

Calm your anger using empathy with these six steps:
1. Notice your feelings.
2. Set an intention for how you want to act and feel.
3. Listen to your assumptions.
4. Listen to your partner.
5. Identify how you think your partner is feeling.
6. Check in with him.

If you do all this and things don't change, consider seeking professional help. There may be more going on than you recognize or understand.

Rule #4: Understand Yourself

Think you're escaping and run into yourself. Longest way round is the shortest way home.

~James Joyce

RULE #4 IS ABOUT understanding and taking care of yourself so you are best able to handle the ups and downs of any relationship. Whenever a client is having a hard time managing their emotional state, I explore physical as well as psychological issues that may be playing a role. If you're not well physically, it is difficult or impossible to be at your best emotionally. In addition to physical problems, if you have unresolved issues from the past, they may also play a role. In this chapter I will cover some basic physical factors that play a role in emotional well-being and then move into psychological issues. The chapter ends with a discussion of accountability, compassion, forgiveness, and knowing your strengths—all of which are part of understanding yourself.

Physical Considerations

Many people have a vague sense that they should exercise, get enough sleep, and eat well, but have no clue as to how beneficial these three "shoulds" are. Often people believe one or more of these are unimportant. Younger people seem to be able to get away with less sleep, little exercise, and a poor diet much more than people can as they get older. They reason if they can live without it and still function, it must not be that important. As you age, you may notice that not getting enough sleep has bigger consequences than it did when you were young. Likewise, poor diet and a sedentary lifestyle may cause you to be less tolerant of certain foods, gain weight easier, feel creakier and slower, and not be as mentally sharp.

Our mental life—our personality, memory, cognition, and spirit—exist in a body. If that body is not operating efficiently or effectively, there will be negative consequences. I don't have to tell you that not getting good sleep affects your ability to think the next day, or that being sick can make doing anything (mental or physical) hard, if not impossible. Most people are keenly aware of how emotional they and others become when they are hungry, upset, or tired. It follows that taking care of your physical needs for sleep, good food, and exercise will improve your ability to handle mentally and emotionally demanding situations.

It is also important to understand your own psychology. What are the things that trip you up emotionally? Where are you vulnerable? What are your strengths? Knowing these will allow you to have a better understanding of how to handle your own emotional state (which I'll get to in Chapter 5). Being aware of your physical needs and limitations, as well as your own psychology, can enhance self-compassion and decrease self-criticism, two important ingredients for psychological health and for functioning well within relationships.

Sleep

One of the biggest myths of our culture is that it doesn't matter if you get enough sleep. People believe they can learn to function on less, but there are big costs to not sleeping well. It's not like training your body to run a marathon or becoming a body builder. Training for these endeavors puts your body through something strenuous and unpleasant in order to build stamina and strength and make it function more efficiently. Sleep doesn't work that way. You can't just slowly decrease sleep time and become more efficient at it.

There are many reasons to be diligent about getting enough sleep. Insufficient sleep has been shown to affect the expression of genes related to immune function, how you handle stress, inflammation, circadian rhythms, and metabolic functions. More recent research has shown that sleep allows the brain to clean out toxins, leading some to speculate that poor sleep may be related to dementia and other neurological problems. For those of you with weight problems or diabetes, poor sleep has been shown to result in an increased consumption of calories.

You only need to meet one two-year-old who has missed his or her nap to have an idea of how a sleep deficit can affect a person's mood and ability to handle stress. Although as adults we are better regulated, we will still suffer the consequences of sleep deprivation. Pay attention to when you and your partner are most likely to get into a disagreement and when you are most able to withstand his annoying behaviors. I'd venture a guess that you are more likely to argue as the day comes to a close. And if he has a few behaviors that drive you nuts, you'll be more annoyed by them at the end of the day. My husband used to try to make me laugh at the end of the day. However, after about nine p.m., I don't find anything funny; I'm too tired. If he tried to make me laugh after nine p.m., we inevitably ended up in an argument. Had he tried earlier in the day, he would have been more successful.

Pay attention to your productivity, moods, ability to handle stress, and predominant thoughts in relation to the quality of your sleep. If you don't have a restful sleep, how does that affect you the next day? I'd encourage you to write it down. Most people I work with are okay after one night of poor sleep, but after two or more nights their productivity decreases, their thinking is more negative, they feel more stressed, and they are moodier. How are your productivity, mood, stress level, and thinking before you go to bed as compared to when you wake up in the morning? Do you need an hour to wake up or an hour to wind down? Pay attention to how your sleep affects you so you can make good decisions about when to deal with difficult interactions. If you have a hard time sleeping, it's worth figuring out what to change to improve your sleep.

Worry will keep you awake at night. Some of my clients worry throughout the day and into the night. If this is a problem for you, make a list of things you are worrying about, even if you have to turn on a light in the middle of the night to do so. Then when your mind wants to worry, you can tell yourself you will address your worry in the morning. You won't have to worry about forgetting about the worry because you wrote it down.

Insomnia

Sometimes you just can't sleep, even though you are not worried or thinking about anything. In this case your body and/or brain is not getting relaxed enough to transition into sleep. A little help may be needed. The first thing to look at is your caffeine consumption. If any client of mine is having problems sleeping, I suggest removing every source of caffeine and other stimulants, regardless of whether you think they're a problem or not. You may not have a problem with caffeine, but if you are having problems sleeping, it's worth making sure. You can always add it back in later.

The next thing to look at is your general sleep hygiene. Make sure your environment is dark, cool, and quiet. Put a bedtime routine into place for the thirty to sixty minutes before you turn out the light. It's best to turn out the light around the same time every night. Consider introducing herbal or aromatic calming agents such as chamomile tea or lavender essential oil. Both are proven to calm the body and facilitate sleep. Another way to calm yourself is to take slow, deep breaths. Breathe in for a count of four, hold for a count of four, exhale for a count of eight, and hold for a count of four. Do this three to six times. Stress causes you to take relatively shallow, fast breaths and creates a slight increase in the ratio of carbon dioxide to oxygen in your blood. Deep breathing sends a relaxing signal to your brain and shifts the carbon dioxide to oxygen ratio back to a calm state.

Help with Sleep
- Write down your worries and worry about them tomorrow
- Eliminate caffeine
- Dark, cool, quiet environment for sleep
- Consistent bedtime routine
- Calming agents, such as herbs or essential oils (try lavender)
- Deep breathing
- Do not argue before bed

Arguing before Bed

I highly suggest making arguments off-limits in the last hour before bed. Make an agreement with your partner to postpone any disagreements until the next day. If you do get into an argument and find yourself keyed up, don't believe you have to resolve the issue before going to sleep. It is an old wives' tale not to go to bed angry. In reality, it's fine to do that. Stop the argument, work on calming yourself down through journaling, deep breathing, and your nightly routine. In all likelihood, you will be calmer the next day and better able to talk through the conflict then.

Exercise

Most people I've met know they need to exercise more, but if they have never felt the benefits of exercise, they don't really believe it. Our bodies were meant to move. Look at your body and what do you see? Under your skin is . . . muscle. What does muscle do? Move. Most of your body is made of structures designed to move: bones, joints, muscles. That is their function. Period. Your muscles, bones and joints want to move. Your metabolic system and your brain are heavily dependent on the energy your muscles expend. In addition, the expenditure of energy through physical activity regulates hormones and neurotransmitters and positively affects appetite, attention, sleep, and your brain.

It's more important to be physically active than it is to work out or exercise. What I mean by physical activity is to move. It could be walking, dancing, riding a bicycle, taking a yoga class, playing tennis or doing any other activity that gets you off the couch and moving. It's best if it is something you enjoy doing. It doesn't have to be a sweat-inducing, heavy-breathing workout. Anything you do is better than nothing.

Most people assume they need to huff and puff and work up a sweat for exercise to count. Don't fall into this trap. I know many people who fail to exercise because sweating and feeling short of breath is uncomfortable for them. They think exercising doesn't count if they don't sweat, and because they don't like to sweat, they never get started. While working up a sweat is beneficial, taking a brisk thirty-minute daily walk is too. Studies show that a daily walk can reduce the risk of cardiovascular disease, improve your mood, and help you lose weight. You just need walking shoes and appropriate attire for the weather. No huffing, puffing, or sweating required!

The nice thing about a thirty-minute walk is that you can practice mindfulness while you're doing it. Doing so will help focus you on the present moment and thereby reduce stress and anxiety. Mindful walking is simple. Focus on how your feet hit the ground, your pace, the way you swing your arms, and how your body feels and moves. Rhythmic movement is very calming, and walking is a great whole-body rhythmic movement. Mindfully focus on the rhythms. You can also focus on your environment, plants, trees, animals, other people, buildings, the sky, etc. Paying close attention to your surroundings will help you forget about your worries and relax you.

Once you are regularly engaging in physical activity, I'd encourage you to try something new, to up your game and do something a little more strenuous. Moderate to strenuous exercise has many health benefits, including improving your mood, reducing your risk of mental illness, improving heart health, and improving cognition, as well as increasing a brain hormone (specifically BDNF, or brain-derived neurotrophic factor) that helps neurons live longer, function more effectively, and is even associated with the creation of new neurons in the memory centers of the brain.

Regardless of whether you sweat or not, strive for thirty minutes of physical activity five days per week or at least 150 minutes of physical activity per week. The benefits to your body will help you be more emotionally resilient and confident. You'll be better equipped to be your best self and conduct your relationship in a healthy manner.

Diet

Diet is a tricky one. It seems like there are endless recommendations about what to eat or not eat and a never-ending stream of new diets to try, not to mention various food allergies, sensitivities, and preferences. People try new diets to lose weight, feel better, or both. Chances are you have done this. Here's the bottom line on eating right: You need to figure out what's right for you by tweaking some basic diet guidelines. Essentially you want to eat healthy food that has been processed as little as possible without eating too much. It doesn't matter if you are vegetarian or carnivore, whether you eat once a day or six times a day, whether you fast regularly or not. It matters that you figure out what works for you.

The metric for what works should be how your diet makes you feel.

The Right Diet for You

A diet right for you should allow you to think clearly, maintain a consistent level of energy throughout the day, and feel sated. These three ways of assessing your diet are important to your ability to function well in relationships. If you are muddle-headed, tired, and hungry, you won't be capable of relating effectively with others. You will be short-tempered, disengaged, and focused on other things—like your next snack or meal.

> **The Right Diet for You**
> - Gives you clear thinking
> - Provides consistent energy
> - Doesn't leave you feeling hungry

Feeling Hungry

Whether you feel full, satiated, or hungry is up to you. Some people believe that going hungry means they are burning fat and losing weight. Unfortunately, the body is smarter than that. If you are hungry because you skipped breakfast or lunch, the hormones that drive you to eat will go into overdrive and you will make up for the calorie deficit later in the day. That's why I discourage people from going hungry. Instead, I encourage clients to pay attention to how they feel as they eat a meal. Rate your fullness when you start the meal, midway through the meal, and again at the end. At the midway point, ask yourself if you are still hungry. If you are no longer hungry, stop eating. If you stop at this point, you will no longer feel hungry and you will not be full. You will be satiated. Eating to the point of feeling full means you've eaten too much.

Are you an emotional eater? It is common to eat foods full of starch, sugar, fat, and/or salt when feeling stressed or emotional. We like these foods because they shift our neurotransmitters and blood sugar levels so we feel calmer. Unfortunately, these foods are not good for us. They cause weight gain, increase blood pressure, and multiply other risk factors for poor health. It's also harder to pay attention to how our body feels when we are stressed or emotional, so we are less likely to heed our body's desire for healthier alternatives. If you are an emotional eater, try substituting a brisk fifteen- to twenty-minute walk or other physical activity for that next slice of cheesecake or bag of chips. Other ways of coping with stress are to talk with a trusted friend, write in your journal, meditate, or engage in a hobby. In addition to these ideas, a longer-term strategy for handling emotional eating is to only keep foods around that you can easily stop eating.

Palatability

Palatability is essentially how much you like a particular food. There are some foods that are harder to resist than others. I have a friend who makes excellent cakes. For me, his cakes are a 9 or 10 on a 10-point scale of palatability. If he gives me a piece of cake, I will eat it and ask for seconds. Likewise, if there is ice cream in my freezer, it isn't there for long. I love ice cream and have a hard time putting it down. Foods like these are not okay to have around if I'm watching what I eat.

I suggest rating foods on a 1 to 10 palatability scale. Foods that you don't like get a score below 5; foods you do like get a score above 5. Pay attention to the palatability of foods and focus on eating foods you give a 6 or 7. Foods in this range are tasty but easier to stop eating when you are no longer hungry than foods rated higher, which you are more likely to overeat. Foods you rate 9 or 10 are also more likely to be less healthy for you. By focusing on palatability you get a two for one: You have more control over how much you eat and on average you'll be eating healthier foods.

Explore ways of eating that are healthy, sustainable, and that support you physically and emotionally. Do some reading on various diets and experiment. Try new things and reflect on how you feel. Talk to others to find out what has worked for them. Get some testing done to see what your health level is (cholesterol, blood sugar, blood pressure, etc.), talk to a nutritionist, make some changes, see how you feel, and get tested again. Making a change like this takes time but the rewards are worth it. You'll feel better, and that will help everyone around you feel better, too.

Other Physical Considerations

Sleep, exercise, and diet are obvious considerations, but since most readers of this book are over forty, it's also important to consider hormonal changes that could play a role in how you feel, both physically and emotionally.

Perimenopause

Most women in their thirties start experiencing a drop in reproductive hormones, even though at first they aren't aware of these changes. They still have regular menstrual cycles and can get pregnant, although their fertility may be declining. By the time a woman is in her forties, the decline in reproductive hormones might be causing noticeable physical, mental, and emotional changes. If she has struggled with premenstrual syndrome (PMS), she may notice more changes or notice them sooner.

Reproductive hormones have a big impact on how the body and brain function. As they start to decline the effects on the body are usually noticeable, but every woman notices something different. For your own emotional well-being, it's important to pay attention to symptoms you may be experiencing and address them if they are causing problems. While the change in hormones alone can cause emotional dysregulation, some of the effects of declining hormones can be quite upsetting (e.g., weight gain, hair loss, wrinkles, etc.) as well. I encourage you to pay attention to whether you are experiencing changes due to perimenopause and consult your doctor if the changes are interfering with your functioning. See the box for a list of common perimenopausal symptoms.

Common Symptoms of Perimenopause
- Irregular periods
- Heavier or lighter periods than normal
- Worsening PMS symptoms
- Breast tenderness
- Weight gain, especially around the belly
- Changes in your hair
- Increased heart rate
- Headaches
- Loss of sex drive
- Forgetfulness
- Problems concentrating
- Muscle aches
- Urinary tract infections
- Urinary incontinence
- Frequent need to urinate
- Hot flashes
- Night sweats
- Fertility issues (if you are trying to conceive)
- Insomnia
- Fatigue
- Anxiety, irritability, depression, mood swings
- Dry skin
- Vaginal dryness

Thyroid

Many women experience changes in thyroid functioning, but this is not a normal part of aging. When the thyroid starts producing too much or too little thyroid hormone many symptoms can arise that affect mood, sleep, metabolism, energy, etc., which can lead to severe health problems. Many symptoms overlap with peri-menopause symptoms, which may delay you seeking treatment. Refer to the box for a list of symptoms and consult with your physician if you suspect a problem. Don't just chalk it up to perimenopause and vow to stick it out. You and your relationships may suffer needlessly.

Symptoms of Overactive Thyroid
- Muscle weakness or fatigue
- Hand tremors
- Mood swings
- Anxiety
- Rapid or irregular heartbeat
- Dry skin
- Insomnia
- Weight loss
- Lighter periods or skipping periods
- Higher frequency of bowel movements

Symptoms of Underactive Thyroid
- Fatigue
- Weakness
- Muscle cramps
- Muscle aches
- Weight gain (or problems losing weight)
- Dry hair
- Hair loss
- Dry, rough skin
- Constipation

- Intolerance to cold
- Irritability, depression
- Memory loss
- Decreased interest in sex
- Abnormal menstrual cycles

The bottom line is to pay attention to your body. If something is getting the better of you emotionally, check in with how you are feeling physically. Don't be afraid to go to the doctor if you notice changes in functioning that linger more than a couple of weeks.

Physical Illness

Although this final point may seem like a no-brainer, I've found it isn't always as obvious as it seems. Being sick or physically compromised in some way, whether with an acute illness such as a cold or the flu or a chronic illness such as diabetes or an autoimmune disorder, will cause a person to be less emotionally resilient. Although a mild acute illness may not keep you from going to work, it may interfere with sleep, affect your appetite, and make you more irritable or impatient. If it gets bad enough you may end up in bed and unable to accomplish even the smallest tasks or relate to others effectively. Chronic diseases such as autoimmune diseases, heart disease, cancer, respiratory illness, kidney and liver disease, and chronic pain conditions, all exact a toll on a person's ability to pay attention to their psychological processes and regulate their emotions. Nearly any physical condition that impacts the body can have a negative effect on your emotional resilience and ability to relate in a healthy manner.

Emotional Issues and Triggers

Emotional problems are part of being human. We all have them, and our emotional reactions stem from two sources unique to each individual: the emotional areas of the brain and our personal experience. As we grow up and go through life our brain develops neural networks in response to what we encounter. Neural networks help us remember what happened and prepare us for responding to similar situations in the future. Each person's neural networks are unique, but they are all built on the same structural foundation. The emotional centers of the brain are the same across all brains, but which emotions a particular individual's brain most commonly experiences will depend on that person's unique history.

The human emotional system is both fragile and resilient. Each person has both the ability to be emotionally injured and to overcome those injuries. Susceptibility to emotional injury is an individual difference—some people are more susceptible than others. Unlike physical injuries, emotional injuries rarely heal on their own. They require some way for the person to put the injury into a greater narrative about who they are and what the injury meant to them.

You will know you have emotional injuries when you react to a situation with more emotion than the situation may warrant. When this happens, even the most successful woman will find herself behaving in ways that are inconsistent with her normal mode of being and possibly with her values. I've seen women who are usually calm and logical become emotional and start crying or yelling. I've witnessed otherwise confident women act out and demand attention if they are feeling ignored. I've seen articulate women lose their voice and quit talking to their partners. All of these actions are the result of emotions taking over and making decisions. This happens because of unhealed emotional wounds.

The first thing to do is to identify those situations or conditions when you are most likely to be triggered. It's part of the process of learning about yourself so you can change your story, heal your wounds, and have more emotional control and resilience. It's going to take some time and willingness to reflect on your behavior, which is not something that comes easily to most people. You may find a trigger you can't resolve on your own. In this case, I'd highly recommend finding a coach or therapist who is skilled in helping people work through being triggered in this manner.

You are probably aware of some situations in which you lose emotional control. It doesn't have to be high drama; losing emotional control could just mean you make decisions you later regret. It could seem like you thought through your decision and acted accordingly, but in hindsight you realized you weren't thinking clearly. Let's start by writing down a description of these situations. There is a worksheet in the appendix you can use for this: Identifying and Processing Emotional Triggers. The worksheet asks you to describe the general situation, how the situation makes you feel, and what thoughts go through your mind. Using the worksheet, write down any situation where you lost your cool or get caught in an obsessive loop. Describe what happened and who was present.

Next list all the ways you felt about the situation. These will be one-word answers, such as scared, disappointed, sad, hurt, angry, etc. It's important to spend some time thinking about all the ways you felt. Emotions are complex and you will feel more than one way about any situation. It's okay to have both positive and negative emotions. For example, if a close friend recently passed away from a painful illness, you may be both sad that your friend died and relieved for your friend because she is no longer suffering.

Finally, list your thoughts in response to the situation. Thoughts will be sentences such as "He/She shouldn't have done that." "How could I have been so stupid?" "If _____ happens it will be horrible." "It was okay for me to do that because . . ." And so on. Just as with feelings, you will have several thoughts for each situation.

Since it can be hard to identify your thoughts, it's important to know a couple of things. First, because these thoughts are automatic, understand that you didn't intend to think them. They're like sneezes—they happen whether you want them to or not. Second, most people aren't aware of these thoughts in the moment. But they are there, and if you stop and consider what you were thinking, you will be able to identify them.

In this first pass at identifying your emotional triggers you will likely get the most obvious ones and miss some of the more subtle ones. Continue to identify them over the next week or so. At the end of the day (or whenever you notice it happening during the day), write down a situation where you felt emotionally derailed, out of control, or overwhelmed. Also consider situations where you realized you made a decision and don't fully understand what you were thinking or why you made that decision. It's possible you were emotionally triggered and not fully aware of it. By the end of the week, you should have a pretty good list of situations that trigger you.

The third step is to review the situations and emotional reactions you've compiled to see if there are any patterns. Which situations show up again and again? Do you have the same feelings repeatedly? Did you notice the same thoughts running through your mind in response to a variety of situations? Can you summarize what you've compiled into a description of a couple of main reactions and repeated thought patterns? It might look something like this:

Common Situations
- Not hearing from _____ when I expect to hear from him (or her).
- He/She is late and makes me wait (or makes me late).

Common Feelings
- Anger
- Frustration
- Disconnection
- Neglect

Common Thoughts
- He/She is ignoring me.
- He/She is angry with me.
- He/She should have allowed more time to get there.
- He/She shouldn't _____.

In this example, there is an underlying theme of feeling disconnected or ignored that leads to feeling angry and frustrated. The thoughts that stem from those feelings are defensive, angry thoughts. Can you see how these feelings and thoughts would lead you to do things that you wouldn't do if you were feeling less threatened and more positive?

Reason for Triggers

Why do we get triggered? Triggers are there for a reason. Your brain has created an automatic response to something threatening. The response has become so automatic that it happens immediately; you have no time to think about it. In the distant past, this was an effective means of keeping you safe. It meant that your body would respond reflexively before you were even aware of a problem. The difference between a trigger and a reflex is that a trigger is created, not built into the system. This means that unlike a reflex, a trigger is not permanent. There are ways to reduce the likelihood and eventually eliminate overwhelming reactions when triggering situations come up.

Self-Compassion and Forgiveness

Now it's time to discuss accountability, compassion, and forgiveness. These skills are important for fixing the problems you are having, whether they are your own personal problems or problems you have with others. Knowing your limitations is important, but you also need to be able to forgive yourself for your limitations and have a good sense of your strengths to be successful at regulating emotions and healing emotional triggers.

When you feel inadequate, are suffering emotionally, or have failed in some way, it's time for self-compassion, self-accountability, and forgiveness. Most people I've met are good with extending compassion to others during times of suffering. They will make a meal for a friend, listen when their friend needs an ear, and tell their friend they understand why they are having a problem. However, we don't extend the same courtesy to ourselves. Instead, we continue to criticize our own behavior, believe we shouldn't be reacting this way, and put ourselves down.

In my discussions with clients about this behavior, they tell me they want to improve. They need to see their faults in order to change them. True enough. I agree with that—you can't fix a problem you don't identify. However, there is a difference between identifying a problem and criticizing yourself for having the problem. When we criticize ourselves, a host of negative emotions is generated, including guilt, frustration, anger, self-hate, etc. These negative emotions cause us to back away from the problem. If you back away from a problem, you aren't engaging with it in a way that will allow you to solve it. You are avoiding it. That's why criticizing yourself for a failure dooms you to repeat the failure.

If you aren't supposed to criticize yourself for faults and failures, then how are you supposed to fix them? The answer lies in accountability, which is a slight variation on criticism. Criticism involves finding fault, judging, or labeling yourself. If you haven't returned your grandmother's phone call and it's been a week, you will feel appropriate guilt. This is something you need to fix. You don't want to ignore people who are important to you. But believing that this failure means you are ungrateful and selfish only enhances your feeling of guilt and drives you further away from making that call. To be accountable is to identify what you did and then find ways of being better next time. It skips the step of creating a meaning that implies you have a character flaw. In this example, you don't assume that your failure to call your grandmother means you are selfish and ungrateful, even if that's the way your behavior looks to others. You recognize that you were distracted or busy and it slipped your mind. To avoid it slipping your mind in the future, you are going to put a reminder in your calendar to call your grandmother every week. Problem solved; no criticism necessary.

> *Being accountable means you skip the step of assuming you have a character flaw.*

Since accountability has not likely been how you approach your flaws, you'll need to find some compassion and forgiveness for yourself. Compassion is essentially treating yourself kindly, as if you are your own best friend. If you wouldn't say it to your friend or you wouldn't want your friend to say it to you, don't say it to yourself. Being human means you are going to get it wrong and make mistakes. You will hurt people. It's inevitable. When possible, apologize and ask for forgiveness. But whether you ask others for forgiveness or not, forgive yourself. Be careful, though: forgiveness doesn't give you a free pass for repeat offenses. The process of forgiveness means to identify what you did wrong and then do your absolute best not to repeat the offense.

What if you have seemingly endless evidence for self-identified character flaws? I have clients who can cite situation after situation that they say demonstrates they are selfish, lazy, stupid, impulsive, etc. Fair enough. Sometimes we identify things about our character we don't like. We know we repeatedly behave in ways we regret. The question remains: What do you want to do about it? If you want a better character, examine the problem, identify what you need to do differently, and start doing it. Beating yourself up about it won't change it. It will only make you miserable and keep you from solving the problem.

✽ ✽ ✽

Congratulations on getting this far. As I've said before, this work takes courage. It is hard work examining your negative emotions and behaviors. Negative emotions are painful and something people naturally try to avoid. Unfortunately, avoiding them only leads to more problems. Instead, we all need to identify and accept our negative reactions. It is only through acceptance of our humanity, including our negative emotions and mistakes, that we gain the space we need to have a choice in how to respond. That space is golden; it is where the magic happens. It is where you assume responsibility for your life, experience your power, and start the process of having better relationships.

Finding Your Strengths

One exercise I ask my clients to do is to write out a list of their strengths and positive characteristics. Almost invariably I get a blank look. They rarely think about what they do right or do well and can't generate a list. Of course if I asked them to make a list of their flaws, they'd have no problem creating a long list of what they believe they get wrong again and again. Does this sound familiar? Can you make a list of what you do right or what your strengths are? If not, keep reading.

The most frequent objection I get when I ask my clients to look at their strengths is a concern about being (or becoming) arrogant if they do so. They believe if they acknowledge or accept what they do well they are being arrogant, so they stay far away from anything that looks self-congratulatory. It's another reason they stubbornly cling to self-criticism. So if knowing your strengths and being able to acknowledge what you do well is not arrogance, then what exactly is arrogance?

Arrogant people believe they are superior to others and have special qualities that deserve to be recognized and admired. They often underestimate other people and devalue the performance of others. Arrogance is not just believing you do things well. An arrogant person desires to be above others, show their superiority, and get recognition for how special they are. You can recognize your strengths without believing you are better than other people and expecting admiration.

Being able to recognize your strengths is also part of self-accountability and self-knowledge. It will help you exercise compassion when you make a mistake. Including your positive characteristics in your self-image gives you a more well-rounded picture of yourself and is important for knowing yourself—just as important as knowing your physical limitations and emotional triggers.

How do you figure out what your strengths are? Well, if you aren't in the habit of acknowledging what you do well, it may be a bit difficult to generate this list on your own. The best place to start is the Three-Word Exercise. For this exercise, email your five closest friends and ask them to give you three words that describe you best. You may feel a little shy doing this, but I've found that people love to be asked. We rarely get the opportunity to tell others all the wonderful things we think of them and how much we appreciate what they add to our lives. A few years back when I asked my friends to participate in this exercise, some of them replied with more than three words. It was as if they were dying to tell me how much they liked me, and three little words weren't enough!

What do you think of what your friends had to say? They aren't lying or exaggerating. This is how they think of you. This is their experience of you. Take this list and put it somewhere you will see it frequently. Feel free to add to it if you think of other strengths and positive personality characteristics.

Refer to this list when self-criticism creeps in. How do your positive characteristics and strengths balance your self-criticism? If you made a mistake or hurt someone unintentionally, what strength can you draw from that may help you address what happened? Have you identified a behavior pattern you don't like about yourself? What strengths can you use in your efforts to change the pattern?

Rule Recap

Rule #4: Understand Yourself

You can't be at your best if you don't feel well. It's important to take care of yourself by getting enough sleep, eating a healthy diet, and being physically active. Pay attention to when you are hungry, tired, or feeling moody, and avoid difficult conversations during those times. Other physical conditions to consider include hormonal changes and physical illnesses, which will make you less emotionally resilient.

Identify your emotional triggers: times when your emotions overwhelm you. There will be patterns in your emotional reactions and thoughts. Be forgiving and compassionate toward yourself when you notice these patterns. Be self-accountable, rather than self-critical. Identify your strengths, make a list, and refer to the list often. Notice your strengths as often as your mistakes.

Rule #5:
Own Your Own
Emotions

Peace. It does not mean to be in a place where there is no noise, trouble or hard work. It means to be in the midst of those things and still be calm in your heart.

~Unknown

Take Responsibility

THIS CHAPTER NATURALLY FOLLOWS from the idea of understanding yourself. Once you know your limitations and emotional triggers, you can start owning—or taking full responsibility for—your reactions. Although your partner, neighbor, family member, coworker, or someone else may have done something that set you off, this is where you stop blaming the other person and tell yourself the truth. This process isn't meant to make you happy all the time. This is the process of taking control of yourself so you have a chance at real

happiness. The flipside of this is only feeling happy when conditions are right and others are treating you the way you want to be treated. There is no control there.

At the beginning of my work with clients, I explain the difference between what we believe is happening and what is really happening when someone responds to a situation. People usually believe that when a situation happens we (or anyone) reacts to the situation.

It looks like this:

> Situation → Reaction

In actuality, this is what is happening:

> Situation → Person → Reaction

The difference is the person between the situation and the reaction. We know that the person between the situation and the reaction is important, because different people react to the same situation differently. If your husband is late coming home from work, you may worry about him and wonder what's keeping him. Your friend in response to the same situation may use the extra alone time to finish reading her book instead of worry. Same situation, different reactions. Thus we can conclude the reaction is coming from a person, not from a situation.

This also means that when people do things, even if they do them in response to something you did, it isn't about you. It's about them. They are the person in this chain of events. You may have created a situation, but the reaction you get out of them says more about their internal processes than it does about you. This is a hard concept to understand; your partner is reacting to something you just said or did. It certainly feels and appears like he reacted to you. But whether he got angry, walked away, or did something else, his response was governed by how he processed the situation (in this case, your words or behavior) and what it meant to him, not by what you said or did.

Likewise, when you react to your partner, he is not making you react a certain way; you're reacting because of how you are processing the situation. This means it is time to stop making your partner responsible for your emotional reactions. It's a hard one, I know. If you've been with your partner for any length of time, he generally has a good idea of how you are going to respond to various situations. He may even do things to "make you mad" knowing you will respond this way. However, he isn't in charge of you—you are. He may do what he believes will make you mad, but it's up to you whether you get mad or not.

Declaring this to be the case is all fine and dandy, but what do you do with it? It certainly doesn't feel like you have much control when your partner does the thing that annoys you to no end—AGAIN! Is your partner chronically late? Do you hate being late? It may feel like he's doing it on purpose just to annoy you, but you don't have to assume that. (Refer to Rule #3: Always Assume the Best).

Instead, you can examine and process your emotional reactions so you don't feel like they are driving the bus. Your partner's tendency to be late will still annoy you, but you will know what to do in response, rather than just repeatedly reacting without much control.

Don't Blame Your Partner

The language we use to talk with our partners about emotions is part of the problem with what we expect from them. We blame others for our emotional reactions. We say "You made me mad" to convey to the other person that their actions or words sparked an angry emotion in us. But those words blame the other person for your emotional reaction. Using those words makes other people responsible for your emotional reaction; it gives them the power and makes you the victim. Start noticing your language, and whenever you blame others, especially your partner, for your emotional state.

While I chose to highlight this process using a negative emotional state, it also holds true for positive emotional states. Catch yourself saying or thinking that your partner makes you happy. This is just the other side of the same coin and just as disempowering. However, we often don't notice when we have this thought about a positive emotion, because we wouldn't "blame" someone for something positive happening.

A situation came up that highlighted my own emotional reaction recently. My father had been having memory problems for the past year. Doctors and family members explored various reasons for his problems and tried various treatments but nothing made a difference. I encouraged my mother to take him to a neurologist, and I called her the day after the appointment to find out what had transpired. My mother told me all about the neurologist sending my dad to physical therapy to address his vertigo (which I didn't know he had), but she didn't mention what the doctor said about his memory problems. I asked her what the doctor recommended for Dad's memory, and she replied that they didn't talk with him about that. I'm usually a very patient person, but that day I became quite angry with her response. Rather than get angry with her, I quickly told her I had to get off the phone. I knew she was doing the best she could. After hanging up, I asked myself, "Why am I so angry?" What was it about the situation that made me so angry? It would have been easy to get upset with my mother for totally missing the point of the appointment and wasting the opportunity to get some answers. But what good would that have done? In looking at why I was so angry, I realized that I felt helpless. My father was not doing well, my mother was apparently not fully up to the task of taking care of him, and I lived too far away to be of much help. If I hadn't stopped and reflected on my reaction, I wouldn't have understood my own sense of helplessness and desire to help. Instead, I would have blamed my mother for not paying attention.

It's reassuring to blame another person for your emotional reaction: While you still feel bad, at least you aren't responsible for it.

Think of a recent situation where you had a negative emotional reaction. Take a moment and stop blaming. Don't say anything about what the other person did, just sit with what happened. Do your best to feel the same negative emotional reaction right now. Identify the emotions you are feeling; focus on yourself, not the other person. Now ask yourself, "Why do I feel _____?" or "Why am I so _____?" Practice doing this whenever something upsets you. It could be another driver, your boss, a family member, or your partner. There are always opportunities big and small to focus on the nature of your emotional reaction and to explore why you had the reaction you did. Practice this frequently throughout the day.

Imagine a scenario where your partner does something upsetting and you are able to separate what he does from how you respond. Instead of flying off the handle or criticizing him, you notice your emotional response and are able to take the time to consider a response that is consistent with your values and how you want to act. For example, when your partner tells you at the last minute that he is unavailable to spend time with you after the two of you had made plans, instead of immediately dissolving into tears and/or getting angry and saying something spiteful, you have a calmer reaction. Although you'd still feel disappointed, hurt, and angry, you'd be able to tell him how his decision affected you

("I'm disappointed that you are no longer able to spend time with me like we had planned.") and then consider your options for doing something without him. Will you still feel disappointed and angry? Yes. But instead of going into attack or criticize mode, you do something to calm down, and don't take it out on him.

When you respond this way, you take responsibility for your emotional reactions and stop putting the responsibility on your partner. He is not responsible; you are. As my clients stop yelling, blaming, and criticizing their partners when they have a negative emotional response, regardless of the situation or who they believe is to blame, an amazing thing happens. They begin to understand their reactions. This is because sitting with your reactions, rather than automatically giving responsibility to your partner, forces you into introspection and shifts you into a different focus of coping. You have to calm yourself down instead of expecting your partner to change his behavior so you can feel better. It's magical. It's also a little difficult to do at first, but it's the only way to give yourself power in the situation.

With a change in your approach to managing your emotional states, you open up the opportunity for your partner to be more considerate of you. Consider this: If you tell your partner in a calm voice that you are disappointed that you won't be able to spend time with him, he may feel guilty and change his plans or determine not to unilaterally change plans in the future. No drama needed. If you are calm when you express yourself and he reacts negatively (e.g., gets defensive) then it is even more apparent that his reaction is his responsibility and not yours. If instead you were angry with him, then it seems more like he's reacting to your reaction.

As you continue to notice your behavior, label your emotional reactions, and ask yourself what you can do better and how you can be more aligned with your values, you will naturally take ownership of your own behavior instead of blaming your partner. This creates space for your partner to own his behavior. Of course, because he hasn't been reading this book and working on this issue, he will probably continue to blame you when he gets upset. That's okay. You don't have to take responsibility.

Once you've been in a relationship long enough, you are bound to feel responsible for your partner's feelings. While you are obligated to treat your partner kindly, you are not responsible for his reactions, just as he is not responsible for your reactions. When he tries to make you responsible for how he feels, don't take responsibility— at least not immediately. Instead, calmly explore with him what his reaction is and why he's having it. You want to find out if you did something that was truly wrong, or if he's reacting for other reasons. Maybe he's had a bad day or he's being overly insistent that you do a task in a particular way or time. If it is one of these situations, you likely didn't do anything wrong, so don't take responsibility for his feelings. If, on the other hand, you did something that hurt his feelings, maybe you do have something to apologize for. I caution you against apologizing just to make him feel better, though. Apologizing for that reason is implicitly taking responsibility for his reactions and reinforcing the pattern of blame.

The Value of Labeling Emotions

I had an opportunity to practice this myself the other day. It isn't a pretty story, but it's perfect for what I have to say next. It was early in the day and due to a couple of small events and a lack of quality sleep, I was feeling more emotional than usual. I couldn't articulate exactly what was going on, but the day started out rough. I was looking forward to getting into the office so I could focus on my clients. That usually helps me calm down and be more centered.

On my commute to the office, there's a short on-ramp that can be a bit tricky to navigate. This particular morning the merge was happening at a normal freeway speed. There was a car slightly ahead of me and a big white Chevy pickup slightly behind me. I determined I could slide between the two and sped up to time the merge. The truck sped up, though, too, and by the time I realized he wasn't going to let me merge, I was at the end of the on-ramp. Fortunately, he changed lanes at the last second and I was able to merge. I don't know if this guy was being inattentive or was the proverbial jerk, but either way, I thought I was about to be in a horrible car accident. I was shaking and yelling, then crying and hyperventilating, all at 50+ mph; not a good state to be in while driving a car.

Let me stop here and point out two things. The first is that my reaction was in response to the white truck not letting me in when I expected him to. Did he create my reaction? No. I could have reacted several ways. I could have gotten angry. I could have followed him down the freeway and gotten into an altercation with him. I could have focused on how it worked out okay even though it was scary in the moment. How I reacted to the situation was all because of my own internal processes, the Person between the Situation and the Reaction.

Second, I needed a way to distance myself from the reaction I was having or I would be putting myself and others in danger. I needed a way out of my reaction. I started a process of labeling what I was feeling.

I thought to myself, "What am I feeling?" I searched for all the words that would capture my overwhelming emotional reaction. What I came up with was alone, helpless, and vulnerable. When I realized those were the three emotions that came up, my first thought was that it was no wonder I was feeling panicky and overwhelmed. Any one of those emotions are enough to knock the wind out of a person. Of course I was overwhelmed. The next thing I realized was I had been feeling all three of those emotions either singly or two at a time quite frequently for the past three years since my husband passed away. During that time I knew I was feeling overwhelmed, but I hadn't broken the overwhelm feeling into its constituent parts. I didn't know I was feeling alone, helpless, or vulnerable. I just thought I was overwhelmed.

Since this incident, I've made a conscious effort to be both compassionate toward the parts of myself that feel these emotions and encouraging of myself to challenge the fear of being alone, helpless, and vulnerable. I know that I am alone in the sense that I'm single. But I'm not alone, because I have friends and family who care about me and would help me out if I asked. I am helpless in the sense that some things happen outside my control, like illness or other people's actions. I am not helpless in the sense that I make good decisions to act with the highest good for myself and others in mind. I may be acting outside my comfort zone, but that isn't being helpless; that's being a little anxious. I am vulnerable in the sense that I could get sick or be in an automobile accident with no warning. On the other hand, I am not vulnerable in many situations; again, I am usually feeling uneasy or anxious. I may be worried that I'll be hurt physically or emotionally, but I'm not actually being hurt, either physically or emotionally. This process of labeling my emotions gave me insight into my own processes and helped me extricate myself from the reaction.

Getting Specific

I have noticed over the years of being a coach that when people start working with me they reach out for help because they are unhappy, they feel "bad." When I ask them to elaborate on what is wrong and how they feel about it, most of the time feeling "bad" is the best way they can describe their feelings. Their ability to articulate the problem causing their bad feelings is usually (a) focused on what others are doing "wrong" and (b) lacks a clear objective for how to make things better. As my clients start to use more descriptive words to describe their emotions, they also improve in their ability to articulate their problem, begin to define what a better situation is, and take responsibility for their part in their situation. It's at this point that things begin to improve. In this section, I'm going to talk about labeling emotions.

Therapists and coaches don't just sit there asking you how a situation made you feel because they were taught to do this (although they were) or because they don't have anything better to say. They ask that question because being specific in your description of how a situation made you feel allows you to start the process of getting to know yourself, learning how to relate to events, and giving you options for how to make things better. You get a better understanding and an improved sense of control over things.

When you label an emotional reaction with a description that is more specific than "bad," you are able to have a discussion about what your reaction means. Why did you feel guilty or angry or sad? What does your reaction say about the rules you have for how to behave properly? What do you think of those rules? Is there room to change the rules? Once you have labeled your emotions, change can start to happen.

If you don't label your emotions, your feelings will be more intense and harder to understand. Emotional reactions that haven't been labeled cause heightened activity in the amygdala, the place in your brain where emotional reactions begin. When you label your feelings you bring other parts of your brain (your prefrontal lobes) to bear on the situation, which help you give meaning to and develop an explanation for what happened. Without the prefrontal lobes' involvement, your amygdala is left to react away unfettered. This makes your emotional reaction more intense and provides you with no interpretation other than the fact that you don't like the way you feel.

Interestingly, when your amygdala gets all fired up, it actually makes it harder for your prefrontal lobes to do their job. If your emotional reaction is intense, your amygdala takes your prefrontal lobes offline. This is why talking about what happened can be so helpful. Not only does the action of talking help to activate your prefrontal lobes and other areas of the brain responsible for rational thinking, but you are bringing in another person and their brain to help out with the process. Since your friend or coach isn't having the reaction you are, he or she is much better at helping you label your reaction and process the situation. Parents do this with small children and we do this for each other every time we sit with a friend or client and let them tell their story.

I have found that it can be difficult to know how you are feeling about a situation when you're in the middle of it, especially if you are just getting started with this whole labeling thing. That's because when you are fired up, you can't think straight; your rational system (prefrontal cortex) isn't looped into the process. But once you have calmed down and are able to reflect on what happened, you will do a better job of figuring out what your reaction was. Having a list of emotion words to help prompt you is tremendously helpful. It doesn't take long before you don't need the list. I've included a list of emotion words in the appendix.

The next time you find yourself feeling "bad," reflect on it a bit after you have calmed down. What just happened? How were you feeling about it? One important note here: You may have felt more than one emotion.

Don't Judge Your Emotion

Once you have labeled your emotions it may be tempting to say, "I shouldn't feel that way" or "I don't want to feel that way" and to judge yourself harshly for having that reaction. Many clients have this reaction about feeling anger. Anger is a strong emotion that encourages people to take action. Unfortunately, when people take action on anger, the action is frequently destructive, which is why it is often discouraged by others. But it doesn't have to be a destructive force. A person can feel anger without acting on it. In this case, the feeling of anger is an important clue to what just happened. It is not in itself a dangerous thing. Acting on it might be dangerous, depending on your impulse, but having the feeling is not dangerous.

Whenever you try to deny how you felt or "decide" that you shouldn't feel that way, you are denying an important aspect of yourself. And here's a newsflash—it won't work. You can't just decide how to feel or not to feel, and you can't just not feel bad emotions. Well, you could try to not feel your "bad" emotions, but if you take that route you will shut down all your emotions, not just the unwelcome ones. I don't recommend it. We connect with others through our emotions and I suspect you are reading this book because you want a better connection. If you shut off your emotions, you won't connect.

As you go through your day and react to things that come up, ask yourself how you feel. What words best describe the emotions that arose? Refer to the list of emotion words in the appendix. Consider looking for two or three words to describe your emotional reaction. It's especially important to do this if your first answer is "I feel angry." When we feel angry we usually stop there, as if that's all there is to our reaction. However, when you are angry you are also having other emotional reactions, not just anger. Anger is a great defensive emotion and it is usually defending you against other emotions such as sadness, hurt, disappointment, embarrassment, vulnerability, and so on. These other emotions are usually deactivating and put us in a vulnerable position. Our angry reaction is actually meant to protect the softer, vulnerable part of us. That's a good thing, but not all by itself. For this process to fully work, you need to identify all the emotions you are feeling. So if anger is your first emotion, keep going and identify one or two other emotions you feel underneath or alongside your anger.

Processing Emotions

Now that you have labeled your emotions, the next step is to come to terms with them. These emotions are there for a reason; they are trying to tell you something.

If you don't pay attention, you'll be missing out on important information about yourself.

There are several benefits of paying attention to your emotional reactions. First and foremost, those especially strong reactions that seem to take over will be less overwhelming. Second, as you learn to listen to your emotional reactions, your confidence will increase. And third, because you are less overwhelmed by your emotions and more confident, you will begin to make better decisions. These benefits will result in improvements in your relationships.

The Observer

Once you have labeled an emotional reaction, you have begun to create a place within yourself that is not overwhelmed by the reaction. This part of you is the observer. The observer is watching the rest of you have a reaction but is not overwhelmed like the rest of you. The more you label your emotions, the more robust this observing part of you becomes. After a while, it will be a rational voice that can start to provide input into how to respond.

I have yet to meet anyone who can be in the middle of an overwhelming situation and use this method to turn the volume down on their reaction as it is happening. It's much more likely that after you have calmed down you'll be able to think back on what happened and the reaction you had.

To start the process of coming to terms with the emotional reactions you've labeled, consider why that reaction came up for you and what it means. For example, if the reaction was one of anger because you were feeling ignored, when else have you felt ignored? What were the conditions that caused you to feel ignored? What do you tell yourself about being ignored? Consider the possibility that you may sometimes feel ignored unnecessarily. Is this one of those times?

These are not easy questions to ask yourself. They require you to take full responsibility for your emotional reaction and not blame the other person, even if the other person said or did something that they knew to be upsetting. Ask yourself the questions in the Processing Emotions worksheet in the appendix. The process of exploring your reaction by asking these questions will help you learn to tolerate the reaction and be less overwhelmed by it.

If you have trouble calming down after a particularly difficult reaction, I recommend the Breathing Exercise for Emotional Overwhelm (see the transcript in the appendix). It takes about two minutes and is highly effective and calming, and it increases tolerance to the reaction. To do the breathing exercise, sit in a comfortable and quiet space and focus on the emotional reaction you are having. It is okay if you are crying or seething with anger or writhing with guilt. Hold onto the reaction and notice where you feel it in your body. Every emotional reaction has a corresponding feeling in our bodies. As it turns out, this is the feeling that we have difficulty tolerating. People are okay with having the emotion of guilt in their head, but when they feel guilt in their gut, they want it to go away now and forever. Find the feeling in your body that corresponds with the emotional reaction you are having. Then begin breathing slowly, deeply, and regularly. Don't hyperventilate and don't run out of air. Breathe at your own pace. As you breathe, imagine your breath is gently stroking that feeling in your body and notice what changes with the feeling in your body. The feeling may move to another place, it may change in intensity, it may change from one feeling to another feeling (e.g., from pressure to heat). After six breaths you should notice that even if the feeling is still there, it is no longer overwhelming. Most people report that the feeling is gone at this point. It's okay to keep breathing beyond six breaths; keep breathing as long as you want.

The reason I'm talking about tolerating the reaction is because we often get into a cycle of having a reaction and then almost frantically doing or saying whatever we can to make the reaction go away. This is when we get into trouble with our behavior or what we say. We have no ability to tolerate feeling. The less we can tolerate it, the more overwhelmed and frantic we become when the reaction comes up. By learning that we are not going to be harmed by the reaction and tuning into what it means or is trying to tell us, we stop being overwhelmed by it. Once we can tolerate it, even just a little bit, we get space to think about how to respond when the reaction comes up. The more we can tolerate it, the more space we have to consider the best response.

Once you have calmed down, go through the Processing Emotions worksheet in the appendix. It would also be helpful to journal about the situation, your reaction, and your answers to questions that explore your reaction. Journaling is another way to include your logical mind in the process of responding to the situation and your emotional reaction.

You Aren't Always Right

Part of owning your own emotions is realizing when you are imposing your rules and your shoulds onto your partner. Shoulds are those ideas we carry around about how we believe things should work. Usually we fail to question whether our beliefs are accurate. We rarely stop to consider whether doing something another way is just as valid as the way we do it. Instead, we assume we are right and that these shoulds are self-evident. If our partner would just pay attention, he would see or understand the importance of doing it our way. Even during those times that we are able to see there is no "right way," we will often persist in imposing our shoulds on our partner just because we are more comfortable with having things done our way.

Unfortunately, if you expect your partner to do tasks your way just because you prefer them done that way, you are setting yourself up for unnecessary arguments. It could be anything from folding towels to making dinner to which route to take to the restaurant. There is no one right way to get a task done. Let's use the example of loading the dishwasher. I've met many people who are particular about how items are arranged in the dishwasher, but the only real rules for loading dishwashers is to give items maximum exposure to water and avoid putting things that might melt on the bottom rack unless you turn the heating element off. If two spoons spoon each other and don't get clean, what's the big deal? Either wash them by hand or leave them in for the next load. Who cares if the bowls go on the bottom rack or the top rack? What does it matter if the dishwasher isn't absolutely full before running it? Arguing about this or a hundred other little things like this (folding towels, driving to an appointments, making dinner, etc.) is unnecessary.

These unnecessary arguments make you feel frustrated or angry and make your spouse feel bad. Why go there when it isn't necessary? This happens most often because knowing a particular way to do something reduces uncertainty. Having other people do it your way also reduces uncertainty, which reinforces the erroneous idea that there is a right way and a wrong way to do something. I think people often lose sight of what's important. It's easy to emphasize efficiency over the effort put into just getting the job done. An example of emphasizing efficiency is that you will have calculated the fastest route to an appointment and expect your spouse to take that route, regardless of other considerations. Being efficient is important, but not at the expense of harmony in a relationship.

Owning your own emotions means, in part, to understand that your perspective is not the only perspective worth considering. Your way of doing things is not the right way. Sometimes we sacrifice too much in an effort to be efficient; we sacrifice harmony in our relationships. I encourage my clients to keep in mind that the vast majority of tasks can be done a myriad of ways, there is no one right way. Recognizing this allows you more space to appreciate your spouse for making the effort. And who knows? Maybe you'll learn something new. The way your spouse wants to do something might surprise you. He may have a better or more creative way of completing the task. At the very least, letting go of these rules, expectations, and should statements will leave you less stressed.

The best way I've found to do this is to let your partner do a task and not to comment or interfere in any way unless he asks you something about it. Then only answer his question and allow him to keep working on the task. When he starts to do something that looks wrong to you, keep your mouth shut but pay attention to your reaction. Remind yourself that he is a smart person and can figure it out on his own. Also remember there is no one right way to do the task.

In the meantime, work on labeling your emotional reaction. Once you've figured out all the labels for your reaction you can work on processing it. I'd also recommend some deep breathing and, if possible, leaving the area where he's working. It's hard to keep from commenting on the work being done by others when it impacts us. If they don't get it done when we think they should or in a manner that feels right to us, it may make us anxious. But that anxiety or stress is yours, not his. This is a perfect way to practice owning your own emotions.

Once the task is finished, notice how he did. Is the task done according to your expectation? If not, consider that the two of you have different definitions of how the task was to be done, rather than conclude that he's being lazy or inattentive. This harkens back to Rule #3: Always Assume the Best. Now you are in a position to talk with him using the effective communication strategy you learned in Rule #1. Tell him what you thought it should looked like. See if he is willing to make corrections.

Household chores and parenting are two common areas of unnecessary conflict that present opportunities to try out your new approach to owning your own emotions. However, I have one caveat: If your partner cannot be relied upon to pay appropriate attention to the safety of your children, then obviously this advice does not apply. Other than safety issues, let your partner parent the children and complete household chores in his way and on his time frame. Process your emotional reactions to his approach and only after the fact use effective communication to let him know what you appreciate and what you'd like to be done differently in the future.

If you are successful at following this advice, keep in mind that you have changed a pattern in your relationship. The change is likely to feel awkward and may cause some anxiety in your partner, as well as in you. Be patient and compassionate toward any reactions and interactions that don't go smoothly. Neither of you knows how to do this new pattern. It's going to feel weird. That doesn't mean you're doing it wrong. In fact, it likely means you're doing something right. At the very least, you did something different.

Handling Your Partner's Emotions

Processing your own emotions is great and everything, but what about handling other people's emotional reactions? This is a big one. One of the most frequent requests I get from clients is to learn how not to react when their partner gets upset. This is always such a big issue. What do you do with other people's emotions?

You've probably had this happen to you: You are in a reasonably good mood when your partner gets home. He's had a rough day and soon says or does something to express his irritation. Almost without knowing why and possibly before he says or does anything, you start to feel a little edgy. His irritation becomes your irritation. Or let's say he's been on the phone with a difficult family member and when he gets off the phone, he tells you about the conversation. In relating what was said, he is more and more expressive of how he feels. In turn, you start to feel upset or agitated. It can work this way on the positive side of things, too, but my clients rarely ask for relief for that.

Our brains are wired to understand other people. That means we need to know their emotional state. This is where empathy starts. Empathy allows us to intuitively know someone's emotional state. It's so important to know this information that we have a whole set of neurons—known as mirror neurons—that are specifically designed to understand others so you can tell whether they are friend or foe. Mirror neurons are what allow us to feel the emotions of other people. If they are happy, we feel uplifted. If they are sad, it brings us down. If they are angry, we feel defensive. You can imagine how important this information would be if you were meeting a stranger at a time in history where strangers could be there to trade with you or kill you.

Unfortunately, because mirroring other people's emotional states is built into our brain, you can't avoid being affected by your partner's emotional state. If your partner has an intense emotional reaction, you will feel it. However, there are ways to reduce the effect so it doesn't throw you off as much.

The best place to start is to examine how you were feeling before his emotional state affected you. With strong negative emotions we sometimes get confused as to whose emotion it is. If that happens we are less likely to respond in a helpful way. Teasing out whose emotion you are feeling will be quite helpful.

One day I was feeling quite productive and somewhat miraculously I also felt like I had enough time to get everything done—not a common occurrence. Just before lunch I met with a client who was feeling under a lot of pressure, as if she didn't have enough time for what was important. We spent nearly the entire hour processing her thoughts and feelings about her schedule and lack of time. After she left my office I sat down at my desk and the first thought I had was that there wasn't enough time to get everything done. Fortunately, I almost immediately realized this was not the case. Just an hour before I had been feeling good about my productivity level and ability to get things done. So where did this thought and the accompanying feeling come from? I had picked it up from my client. Because I was feeling her stress, I knew I had to do something other than sit at my desk to relieve myself of this feeling, so I went for a quick walk around the block. It worked like magic and I was back to my previous feeling of ease.

Using this example, let's examine a situation you may experience. Imagine you were doing just fine until your partner walked into the room feeling upset about something. If you weren't upset before he walked in and now you are, then that feeling is most likely his feeling. Because it is now in your brain and body it may feel like it is yours, but it isn't necessarily. Go off by yourself for a few minutes and think about where that feeling came from. Is it possible that it doesn't belong to you? If you develop your skill in identifying when an emotional state is coming from another person, you can get a little distance from it and be able to empathize with their situation.

What if, in addition to having an intense emotion, your partner is blaming you for his emotional state? This isn't uncommon. Imagine your partner is tired and irritable when he gets off work but isn't paying attention to how he feels. As a result he may feel as if the first thing you do that he doesn't like is what is causing him to feel irritable, when in fact he was irritable before he walked in the door. Since he wasn't paying attention to how he felt before he got home, he believes that you created this state in him.

You know from our earlier discussion of owning your own emotions that you did not create this state in him, but he doesn't know that. This is where your new skills of labeling your emotions and understanding mirror neurons is going to come in handy. It will help you distance yourself emotionally from his belief that you are the cause and respond in a (mostly) neutral way, even if you start to feel annoyed with him.

This won't be easy initially. But I'd encourage you to go through the process of labeling your emotions and examining your thoughts and behavior as I outlined above to figure out your responsibility. Realizing that he was irritable before he walked in the door will help you have confidence that you didn't do anything to warrant his accusation. Knowing you aren't responsible for his emotional state will help you stay more neutral when he begins to blame you. The interesting thing about being able to stay neutral is that it makes his incongruous emotional state more obvious. If he's irritable and you aren't, then he looks more like he's the one with the problem, which he is. If you respond to his irritation with your own irritation, then it confuses the situation and makes it a lot easier for him to blame you for how he's feeling.

Rule Recap

Rule #5: Own Your Own Emotions

Reactions come from people, not situations. Your partner does not make you react, just as you do not make him react. By no longer blaming your partner for your reactions, you open up space for him to make changes. You are also likely to stop taking ownership of his emotional reactions, even if he blames you.

If your partner blames you for how he feels, explore his reaction and only apologize if you did something that calls for an apology. Don't apologize just to make him feel better, as doing so is implicitly taking ownership of his emotional state.

Labeling emotions will help you get some emotional distance from them and start the process of gaining an ability to respond, rather than react.

If you don't like the way you reacted, explore why you had that reaction, rather than making yourself wrong for it. If you believe you shouldn't feel that way, it's going to be more difficult to figure out why you had the reaction in the first place and then do something about it.

Do the breathing exercise in the appendix if you need help calming down after having a reaction.

Be on guard for unnecessary arguments. There is often more than one way to do a task, so don't make your partner wrong for doing it a different way than you do it.

It's easy to react to other people's emotions because of how our brains are structured. Be aware of whether your emotional state is coming from your partner.

Rule #6:
The Past Plays a Part, but the Present is Primary

*Though no one can go back and make
a brand new start, anyone can start from now
and make a brand new ending.*

~Carl Bard

Past vs. Present, Changing the Patterns

IF YOU HAVE BEEN (or were) married for a number of years, you may have noticed patterns in your relationship that never seem to change. You have the same old arguments, the same feelings in response to his annoying habits, the recurring sense that you know what he will say or do. It seems like you are responding to him, but you are actually responding to the pattern. Remember what I said in Rule #5: Own Your Own Emotions about reacting to situations rather than people? Although it seems we react to people, we are really reacting to situations based on our past, our expectations, our assumptions, and our beliefs.

Women whose marriages or partnerships have ended and who have gone on to date other men will know what I'm talking about here. These women tell me how surprised and frustrated they get when they react to their new partner as if he was their ex-partner. They often lament finding men that are eerily similar to their exes, men who talk and behave in unsettlingly similar ways.

They know that their new partner is not the same as the last partner, but a primitive part of the brain doesn't make that distinction. All it knows is that this important person has said or done something that reminds them of the past. Once the association has been made, it almost doesn't matter who started it; it feels the same.

Our brains are superb at recognizing patterns. It's how we identify faces or feel as if we know what is about to happen. Learning patterns is how habits are formed and skills are mastered. Any pattern your brain learns is essentially a network of neurons that fire together. Sometimes that network includes emotional reactions, specific comments, or automatic behaviors. It doesn't matter what sparked the activation of the network. It could be your husband making annoying comments for the umpteenth time or your new partner sounding a little like your old partner. The pattern gets activated and it feels the same.

This is how the past plays a part in our interactions, but it's vital for us to focus primarily on the present, on what is happening right now. It's easy to go with the flow and engage with your partner without paying attention to the fact that a pattern from the past has been triggered. Unfortunately, the pattern that was triggered in you may have little to do with the present moment. The brain operates so quickly, it may have jumped to a conclusion without taking all relevant information into account. It just sees the slightest hint of a familiar pattern and the whole network lights up.

One observation I've made about changing these habitual patterns of interaction is that you cannot fix them on your own; another person needs to trigger you. When a pattern is triggered it will include a cascade of emotions that you can't generate simply by thinking about past instances of the pattern. You need to be able to interact with another person in real time to confront and change those patterns.

You may no longer be in a relationship with the person or people who created the conditions that formed the patterns you want to change. But as long as you have a pattern that needs to be addressed, there will likely be someone out there who will trigger the pattern and give you an opportunity for growth. Your job is to be mindful of your behavior so you can identify old patterns when they crop up.

It is hard to see our own issues, but a trusted friend or coach can point out what we are doing and the pattern they see. A coach is better than a friend because a coach is not emotionally involved with you the way a friend is. You don't have to worry about any allegiances or motives a coach may have, but regardless of whether you're working with someone on this or doing it yourself, the basic idea is to notice the pattern, break it down into its parts, identify the parts you have control over, and decide how you'd rather respond. Then when you notice the pattern happening in real time, refer back to how you decided to respond in order to change the pattern. From that point on you can tweak your responses: Each time the pattern is triggered, you get another opportunity to respond more effectively.

If You Are Single or Newly Married

The unsettling part of dating after being in a longterm relationship is reacting to your new partner as if he were your previous partner. If your previous relationship had problems you want to avoid repeating but you're running into the same patterns, this can be rather disturbing. You might wonder whether you are doomed to repeat the same problems you were trying to avoid. With a little work, though, avoiding a repeat of the problems you most want to avoid is doable. You just need to pay attention to your responses and have a way to change the patterns.

The good news is that your new partner is not the same person as your old partner. Even if he triggers an old pattern in you, in all likelihood he will respond differently to you if the pattern starts to play out. Because he doesn't know your old pattern, he won't do or say the same things your past partner did, which will help you notice and break the pattern.

If You Are in a Long-Term Marriage or Partnership

If you are still married, you are undoubtedly aware of various patterns and routines in your marriage. Any relationship is like a dance between two people. Relating to another person will become a pattern of interactions between the two of you that gets repeated over and over again. If you move one way, he will predictably move a specific way in response. This is how you stay in the relationship. If you are doing the swing and he wants to square dance, you can't dance together. Since you are still in the relationship, you are both still engaged in the same dance.

In one sense you are reinforcing your partner's behavior by responding to him, and he is reinforcing yours. The dance has become habitual, which makes it hard to change, but not impossible. Your partner is unlikely to be aware of the pattern and therefore not likely to change his behavior initially. He will be engaging in the pattern but you won't be following along as usual; it will be like trying to change the dance. You may metaphorically step on each other's feet. It will feel awkward at first and you may not initially get the results you are after, but be persistent.

The key to changing the pattern within you and between you and your partner is a culmination of all the things we have learned so far. Let's review what we've learned and how it applies to changing habitual ways of interacting.

Rule #1: Tell the Truth

We established in Rule #1 the importance of telling the truth. The most important person to tell the truth to is yourself. If you aren't willing to examine your patterns and own your part, there is no footing for change. Likewise, you need a way to communicate honestly with your partner. This is where effective communication comes into play.

Single

Learning how to communicate effectively with someone you aren't familiar with can be challenging. You don't necessarily know what he expects or whether he will communicate his truth back to you in an effective manner. Hint: Most people won't be effective communicators or know what their truth is.

Married

Opening up about the truth as you see it can be jarring for your long-term partner. If you haven't been honest with him about your feelings or experience of the relationship in a while, he won't be expecting what you have to say. You may try using effective communication strategies, but if he's confused, it may seem as if the strategies aren't all that effective. Hang in there. You may need to repeat your message a few times, but he will eventually come to understand your position.

Rule #2: Believe Him When He Shows You Who He Is

This is an extension of telling yourself the truth. You need to take an honest look at your partner's behavior and draw a truthful conclusion about how it affects you without making a lot of excuses for him. When you make excuses for his behavior, you effectively discount what you want and deserve from the relationship.

Single

The best time to start looking at the truth of someone's actions is early in the relationship. If undesirable behavior shows up early, you better believe it will be worse later on. That's because people are usually on their best behavior initially. Their undesirable behavior doesn't usually come out until they relax in the relationship a little bit. So if behavior you don't like or aren't willing to allow in your life shows up early in the relationship, it's important to confront it.

Married

If you are in a long-term relationship, ending the relationship is a last resort. Therefore, telling yourself the truth of his actions is harder and can destabilize the relationship in a much different way than if the relationship is new. It's harder because it may mean confronting some ugly truths about the nature of your relationship. Once you confront the truths within yourself, it can destabilize the implicit agreements or patterns you have established that keep the relationship intact. It's also important to note that once you are in a relationship with established ways of thinking about your partner's behavior, it's hard to tell whether you are seeing his behavior for what it is. Our expectations and assumptions cloud our judgment. This is where an objective third party like a coach or therapist may come in handy, because as you can tell, if there are hard truths to confront it won't be easy.

This paints a rather bleak picture, but things might not be that bad. It depends on the nature of your relationship and how truthful you've been with yourself and your partner.

Rule #3: Assume the Best

Always assume the best-case scenario to explain your partner's actions. We are poor predictors of the motivations and intent of other people, even if we know them well. That is because we do not generally understand the situation someone else is in. Because you have to make up some information about why your partner did something, you may as well make up favorable information, rather than information that paints him in a bad light. You can always correct yourself later, but assuming the worst harms the relationship. It communicates that you don't trust him or don't feel you can rely on him.

Single

In a new relationship it is a bit easier to assume the best because you are not caught up in established patterns. Even so, be aware of any tendency to assume the worst. If he doesn't call you back right away, do you assume he got busy or distracted, or that he doesn't care about you and the relationship is doomed? Your initial reaction can give you some insight into your patterns and what may need to be changed in your thinking.

Married

This is a hard one if you have a habit of assuming the worst. Let's say your partner is late coming home from work, even though he promised to be home on time. Let's further assume that he does this regularly. It might be reasonable to assume that he doesn't care about what you want enough to make an effort—but believing that he doesn't care about you makes you feel bad. If instead you assume he's working hard to make sure he keeps his job and earns money for the two of you, you'll have an easier time dealing with his lateness. Your ability to shift from worst-case scenario to something more benign will improve the more you work on it.

Rule #4: Understand Your Limitations

Understanding how your physical state affects your ability to engage in a healthy way is important when relating to anyone. If you are hungry, tired, sick, or in pain, your ability to be engaged will be compromised. Likewise, past emotional patterns or triggers can affect how you relate to others. Know your limits and your triggers.

Single

Gaining insight into your patterns and making changes is vital if you want a different relationship the next time around. However, gaining insight is just the first step. You won't have much success actually changing the pattern until you are confronted with opportunities to change in the context of a relationship. Once you have a new relationship, you can practice being open with your new partner about your patterns and elicit his help in changing them.

Married

The great thing about learning how your physical state and past emotional patterns affect you is that you will also be able to see how these factors affect your partner. You will be able to see how being hungry or tired affects his mood and patience. This may give you room to be more compassionate and make positive assumptions about him and how he interacts with you. It also offers you the opportunity to be compassionate with yourself when you get sucked into old patterns of behavior before you are able to stop yourself.

Rule #5: Manage Your Emotional State

Once you have an understanding of your limitations (both physical and emotional), you're ready to start the process of managing your emotional state. First, label your emotions, then consider where they came from and how you'd prefer to react. (For help, see the Processing

Emotions Worksheet in the appendix.) Learning to tolerate your difficult emotions without acting on them is key. If you can manage your state in difficult conversations you will have a much better ability to respond in a healthy way. This is the same whether you are single or married.

You can use the breathing exercise for emotional overwhelm. There is a transcript in the appendix.

You Have to Change First

Now let's consider a situation where you have a problem with your partner. It doesn't matter whether you are partnered or just dating. Let's say you don't like a habitual behavior he has, such as being late, spending too much time on his smartphone, or always expecting you to make dinner. It could be anything. My question to you is this: Who has the problem?

Of course he has the problem, because if he would just change his behavior a little bit, then you'd be happier and feel more connected to him.

But is it so obvious that he is the one with the problem? After all, an intelligent adult who has a problem would generally do something to fix the problem. So if he has a problem, why hasn't he fixed it? The unfortunate truth is that he doesn't have a problem. You do.

You are the one who is upset and you are the one who wants something to change that you have no control over. That's a problem.

One could say that if he really loved you and you were upset about something, he'd figure out how to fix the problem so you weren't upset anymore. But since you've complained and he hasn't fixed the problem, then we can conclude he doesn't believe he has a problem. He may believe you are being overly dramatic or unreasonable, but he doesn't believe he has a problem. He (rightly) believes you have a problem.

As you do the exercises in this book and start practicing the rules, you will begin to change. Things will become obvious to you that then seem *so* obvious you believe anyone else should see them too—especially your partner. But it doesn't work that way. If you grow a bit and expect your partner to change along with you, you will be sadly disappointed. People grow at different rates. We are open to information at different times in our lives. You're open to this information now and it's making a difference. But your partner might not be as open as you are and won't be growing in the same way. That means he might continue to do things the old way despite your suggestions or requests to the contrary.

While you read this book to create a better relationship, it may seem at first like you are taking steps in the wrong direction. If you grow a little and he does not, the gulf between you may seem wider and harder to cross. Hang in there. The two of you are in a dance, and if you change the steps of the dance, he will need to make some changes in response and that takes time.

The other thing about the idea that you have the problem and not him is that you have to change first. This is a hard one for many of the women I coach. Women who have been married for a while have usually been quite clear about what they'd like their partners to do differently and have been asking for years. They begin to believe that their errant partners owe them something; their partner needs to do some changing. While it may be true that their partners are not participating in the relationship in a healthy way and should make some changes, the partners don't usually believe they have a problem and therefore they have no incentive to change. But they're not the one that needs to make the first move. You need to change first.

It can be difficult to come to terms with the idea that you need to change first. But remember, you can either insist on being right, which you might be, or you can move toward a happier relationship. Which do you want?

The Present is the Only Place of Control

Since you have to make the first move, which move do you make? I'd suggest starting small and working your way up. Here are places to look.

Overreacting

It's hard to be present when the past is in play in a negative way. Past experiences play into our emotional reactions nearly every time we react to something. For example, if meeting new people is hard for you, then going to a party where you don't know anyone would be torture. You may find it odd that other people enjoy this activity. Usually past experiences guide us; they help us know what we are comfortable with and what bothers us. They inform us how to behave. In relationships, however, we are usually confronted with a partner whose past experiences are unlike ours. They don't find the same things objectionable and they do things we find objectionable.

I have a friend, Anthony, who grew up in an Italian family. In this family whenever there was conflict there was a lot of emotional expression. Anthony's partner, Pat, grew up in a family where conflict was avoided at all costs. Now when they have a disagreement Pat feels as if Anthony is yelling, and Anthony can't understand what the problem is. He doesn't feel he is yelling. This level of emotional expression feels normal to him, but it feels completely over-the-top to Pat. Pat feels that Anthony overreacts to most situations.

Have you ever been accused of overreacting or wondered if you were doing so? It's an interesting label to put on an emotional reaction.

Emotional reactions tell you something about the situation you are in. Your reactions might tell you that you are in charge, or feeling threatened, or enjoying yourself. They are not good or bad; they just are. But it's common for one partner to accuse the other of overreacting. It's such a common accusation—one we even impose on ourselves—that I think it is important to consider what it means.

When someone accuses you of overreacting, or if you wonder whether you just overreacted, you are likely noticing that your reaction is somehow out of proportion to the situation. It may be. Sometimes it is hard to tell, especially if you are reacting to your partner doing something for the umpteenth time that you cannot stand. In this case, some portion of your reaction is related to the present, but most of your reaction is coming from the past, from the hundred other times he did the same thing. You are a hundred times as irritated as you would be if this were the only time it happened. Your reaction is out of proportion to the current episode, but not out of proportion if you take into account all the past episodes.

The answer to the question of whether you overreacted is both yes and no. Yes, you overreacted if we only consider the current episode. No, you didn't overreact if we take into account all 101 times the same thing has happened.

Can you see how the past can influence your reactions in the present, and why it can be hard to stay present? When the same episode happens for the hundredth time, staying present is hard.

This is a perfect example of how difficult it is for others to see your situation. (See Chapter 5.) Your partner may only see you react to this instance, forgetting (or ignoring) all the other times he's done the same thing. The current instance is obvious, the previous one hundred instances are not obvious.

The importance of understanding how your past influences your present cannot be understated. This is part of understanding yourself and owning your own emotional reactions. If you find yourself overreacting, you are likely experiencing an intrusion of the past into your present. Figure out the assumptions your brain is making, work on identifying your emotional trigger, process your emotional reaction, and throw in a little self-compassion.

Overdoing or Overgiving

Another area that needs to be addressed is the area of overgiving or overdoing. Overgiving is common in people who believe they are not worthy of a relationship. Because they want a relationship they attempt to ensure or cement one by bending over backwards and going out of their way to do things for the other person. They are always available, give gifts, make offers, make suggestions, and are flexible when making plans. They try to always be available and understanding. They assume they are the reason their partner is either upset or avoiding them. In essence, they take too much responsibility for the nature of the relationship.

I believe this is one of those patterns that stems from rules learned as a child. The rule is if you are kind and giving, you will get what you want and need from others. This rule works really well for other people and you likely got huge reinforcement for functioning this way in relationships. While this approach has a lot of merit, it only works in moderation. If overdone, it leads to being taken advantage of. If you are an overgiver or overdoer, you likely feel in some relationships you have been taken advantage of.

If your partner asks you to do something, you are willing to do it, even if you have to rearrange your entire day to do so. You go out of your way to do things for him, but he doesn't appreciate your efforts. Sometimes you don't even get credit for having done the work. This pattern can show up in nearly every area of your life, so if you think this isn't you, look at your friendships, family relationships, and work life, too. Do you get credit for the amount of effort you are putting in? If not, you are likely overgiving or overdoing.

While it is okay in some instances to be an overgiver or overdoer, it doesn't generally pay off in your intimate relationships. Initially it may make it easier for the relationship to develop, but ultimately it will lead to you taking on too much responsibility, giving your partner too much slack, and not getting what you need out of the relationship.

The key to ending this pattern is to back out slowly. Start by being truthful with yourself about what you are putting into the relationship and how much responsibility you are taking for the relationship. Then identify a few small areas where you can start to set limits and say no. Do this even if it seems arbitrary.

I did this with my husband; I usually worked with him in the yard on the weekends. Sometimes he wouldn't feel like mowing the lawn and would ask me to do it. I always felt like I should do it because he asked me, but I didn't want to mow the lawn. Since there were tasks I always did because he either wouldn't or couldn't do them, I realized I didn't have to mow the lawn. I started refusing to do it. Every time he asked, I said no. It felt very weird at first. I knew I could mow the lawn. I had the time and the skills, but I also knew that I needed to start saying no more often, so I picked this arbitrary task and began to refuse. Over time, I became more comfortable with saying no and extended my boundaries to other tasks and issues.

If you aren't sure where to start with this, reread the list of rights under Rule #1. Where are you giving up rights to keep conflict to a minimum? This might be an area to start saying no. Pick small issues to get some practice before you move onto bigger issues. Your partner is used to you saying yes, so there may be some pushback. It's better to flex your no muscle on little things before tackling bigger things. If your partner pushes back against your no, you can practice the effective communication skills from Rule #1 to let him know that you understand what he wants but you aren't available right now.

Another area to examine is your desire for a relationship versus your partner's desire. If you get the feeling that you want it way more than he does, if there is an imbalance there, you are likely overgiving. Again, back out slowly. Stop being so available, and start asking him for things. Start slowly. Maybe you don't answer the phone when he calls and you call him back ten minutes later. Even something as small as that might make you uncomfortable; if so, that's a good place to start. What if you miss him? Chances are, the consequences will be so minuscule that it won't matter. What if he wants to plan an outing, but is vague on the details so he can "see how the day develops"? This is a recipe for you waiting around for him to finish what he's doing before you get together, but who knows when that will be? If he can't be specific and you go along with that, you are overgiving: being too flexible with your time. Next time he does that, let him know that you will be available at a specific time. If he is not available at that time, then you will be off on another project.

When to Stop Trying

If you've been in a relationship for a while and truly love your partner, when do you decide that the conflict is no longer worth tolerating? After all, some conflict is inevitable. How long do you live with behavior you don't like, that makes you feel disconnected or disregarded—or worse? This is a hard question to answer. Every couple is going to have their own problems and each person in the couple is going to have different abilities to deal with conflict.

If you are unhappy and have asked for change, but change does not happen, then you may start to consider leaving the relationship. If the conflict is bad enough, if it could be called abusive, then ending the relationship may ultimately be in your best interest.

Even if you feel the relationship has become abusive, stop to consider whether something else may be going on. Sometimes we reach a point where we feel we are being abused, but our partner has an addressable issue that has prevented him from changing his behavior.

Problems such as unrecognized physical ailments or mental health problems (depression, anxiety, substance abuse, ADHD) can create untenable situations in relationships. In general, these problems are fixable and addressing them can have a dramatic impact on the dynamic of the relationship.

Is It Abusive?

When does perpetual conflict cross the line into abuse? This is an important question. I've met several wonderful people who have been in relationships where they were being emotionally or physically abused and they didn't know it. They didn't label the interactions as abuse.

People often fail to recognize abuse that doesn't involve hitting, but physical abuse includes grabbing, blocking the way, and pushing. Victims of emotional and verbal abuse don't necessarily understand they are being abused, either. They believe they have done something wrong to upset their partner, and if they changed their behavior, their partner wouldn't act that way. They take responsibility for their partner's angry reaction by telling themselves they shouldn't have done what they did.

Verbal and emotional abuse violate most, if not all, of the rights outlined under Rule #1 in the section regarding effective communication. They tend to blame the victim for the state of the relationship and therefore the abuse. Please refer to the appendix for more information about abusive relationships; I have included resources that will help you figure out if this is what you are dealing with.

If you are experiencing any form of abuse, you need professional help to address the interaction. Women who are being abused physically or emotionally are at great risk of physical harm if they try to leave the relationship. If you feel you need to get out, I urge you to stay as safe as possible and to find a professional who has expertise in abusive relationships to help you.

If you've been in an abusive relationship in the past, use your past to help you recognize when someone is engaging in abusive behavior with you now. In this way the past will serve you. This gets back to the issue of red flags and being truthful with yourself about the effect of someone's behavior on you. Rather than giving someone a second chance or the benefit of the doubt (again!), maybe it's time to call a spade a spade and not pursue the relationship when abusive behavior appears to be present.

Rule Recap

Rule #6: The Past Plays a Part, but the Present is Primary

Our brains are superb at recognizing patterns and will often recognize and react to an old pattern from a past relationship, even though a different person triggered it.

The first 5 rules will help you change patterns after you have identified them.

1.   Tell the truth using effective communication
2.   Believe him when he shows you who he is
3.   Assume the best
4.   Understand your limitations (and be aware of his)
5.   Learn to manage your emotional state

Realize that you have to be the one to make the first changes because you are the one with the bigger problem.

If you've overreacted to a situation, this an opportunity to identify an emotional trigger and an old pattern.

If you are an overdoer, start by telling yourself the truth and then making small changes, such as saying no to minor things, even if you don't have a "good enough" reason to say no.

If you have tried the advice in this book and you have asked for change but nothing is changing, consider getting professional help. If the relationship has become abusive, getting professional help is even more important.

Rule #7:
Above All Else,
Be Kind

The more we genuinely care about others,
the greater our own happiness and inner peace.

~Alan Lokos

When the Rules Don't Apply

LIFE AND RELATIONSHIPS ARE complicated. If they weren't, you wouldn't be reading this book. If life and relationships came with a manual, it would all be easier, but they don't. People are complex, situations are complex, and when people and situations are combined in relationships, the complexity is multiplied many times over. It is impossible to cover every scenario or question with these six rules, so I've added a seventh rule for the times when the rules conflict or don't apply. You may have learned early in childhood that there is an exception to every rule. (Remember learning to spell and being told that i comes before e, except after c?) Being flexible and adaptable with individual people and situations is key.

Rule #7 is meant to guide you when you aren't sure how or whether to apply the rules. If you are being honest with yourself about the effect of someone's behavior and trying to always assume the best about them, it is highly likely that at some point your assessment of their behavior and your assumption that they are doing their best will conflict. Likewise, how do you power through with empathic understanding when you've run up against your limitations and emotional triggers? How do you separate out influences of the past while striving to tell the truth and avoid negative assumptions? What if your negative assumptions about your partner turn out to be true? Then what?

In real life it can be difficult to know how to handle each situation, but being angry, mean, or vindictive—no matter how hurt you are—serves very little purpose. At the very least, being kind leaves you on high ground with your integrity intact.

Being Kind

Most people believe that being kind means being polite and saying or doing things that leave another person feeling good. While that is one way to be kind, it is not the only way.

The dictionary says that to be kind is to be gentle, caring, and helpful. It also says that to be kind is to have a friendly, generous, and considerate nature. Let's combine these two definitions to create a more comprehensive definition: To be kind is to be caring and helpful in a way that is gentle, friendly, generous, and considerate. Ultimately, to be kind is to be caring and helpful.

Let's back up and think about what the purpose of being kind is. Kindness is a way to express common humanity. It means knowing that life is hard for everyone and that kindness makes it a little easier. It means improving a person's circumstance in some way. When we think of improving a person's circumstance, we think of giving them food, money, a ride, or some other form of help. Or we think of pointing out what they are doing well, rather than what they got wrong. But doesn't it also improve a person's circumstance if we help them do better for themselves? It's the idea of teaching a man to fish, rather than just feeding him. If a person is capable of doing something for him or herself, then teaching them how to do it is far kinder than doing it for them.

Being kind is not just about being nice. Being nice is to treat people well and to be polite. It is quite possible to be nice without being kind. For example, it would be nice to compliment someone on how great they look, but your compliment would lack kindness if you failed to point out they had spinach in their teeth. Just complimenting them is polite and makes them feel good, but it is rather unkind not to point out something they could easily fix, they don't know about, and would embarrass them later. This may seem like a trivial example, but if you're the person with spinach in your teeth, how do you feel later when you discover that no one you've seen all day has told you? It's quite possible you will feel a little angry.

For all you people-pleasers out there—and many if not most of us fall into this behavior to some degree— being kind does not mandate that you let other people tell you what to do, demand things from you, or take advantage of you. Over the years I've had repeated conversations with self-labeled people-pleasers who have come to the realization that others have been taking advantage of their kindness. When they try to figure what to do differently, it seems to them that saying no or setting boundaries is the opposite of being nice or kind. They think it's rude or mean.

Well, it is not rude to say no or to set boundaries with people. If you fail to do these things, you are being unkind to yourself. You are not taking care of yourself or being considerate of your own needs when you put the needs of others ahead of your own all the time. Failing to take care of yourself is going to have negative consequences for you—and for everyone else in your life, too.

Here is where we run into a conundrum. How do we do for others without overdoing it? Doing things for others is a lubricant of social life. It makes everyone's lives a bit easier. It fosters relationships and keeps people together. Otherwise, we'd all just be individuals living and working in the same space with little else keeping us together. But we can overdo it, and that's what people-pleasers run into: How can they balance helping others without being taken advantage of?

We do for others because we feel it is in the best interest of the other person and ultimately in our own best interest. The other person gets the benefit of being helped, and if you help enough other people, then you'll get what you need in return. But let's examine the idea of "in their best interest." We'll focus on adults, because what's in the best interest of children is a different matter, although sometimes we act as if there is little difference and treat adults as if they are children.

What is in someone's best interest? For mature, healthy adults, it's to be able to tell the truth and behave in a manner that helps themselves and others at the same time. What is in my best interest is also in your best interest today, next month, and next year. If you and I are in a relationship and I make a decision in my best interest, whatever I decide will be in my best interest only if it is also in your best interest now and into the future. For example, a client of mine recently realized that she craves spending time alone. She has never demanded alone time because she felt selfish for not allowing her family members access to her when they felt they needed her. She felt like she would be ignoring them. One result of not getting her much-needed alone time is that she became angry and resentful at her family members for demanding her time and attention. She was doing a lot for others, but not getting what she needed in return. As you can see, this serves no one. Under this scenario, my client doesn't get her alone time and her family doesn't get a loving wife and mother.

My client came to this realization as she confessed to me her negative feelings about her family members and the private time she wanted. Her confession and solution felt to her like she was violating what she was supposed to be: a loving, caring wife and mother. I pointed out to her that following her rules for being kind wasn't resulting in the type of person she wanted to be. She didn't feel good about herself and her family didn't feel good about their relationship with her.

We had discussed all the rules and she had been working at applying them. She'd made good progress in understanding herself and telling herself the truth, but then she came to a sticking point. How did all that understanding of herself translate into saying no and setting boundaries with her family? She felt that the rules either didn't apply to what she needed to do or they conflicted with each other. This is where Rule #7 comes in.

We just determined that the definition of kindness is doing what is in everyone's best interest. What was difficult for my client was that she had to start saying and doing something she feared her family members wouldn't like. She felt she was being rude and selfish and expected that her family members would be upset with her. All this felt like the opposite of being kind. But once she realized that she had confused being kind with being nice, things got a little easier. Being nice meant she didn't have the freedom to say things that might upset her family members, but being kind doesn't have the same restrictions. She could ask that she not be disturbed because she was going to go read her book and it didn't mean she was being rude.

If she did what was in her best interest, it would ultimately be in the best interest of her family members. In the short term it could mean that she didn't watch television with her family in the evening. Her son might have to get a ride home after going to the movies with friends. Her daughter might have to fix her own dinner if she wasn't home by dinnertime. These changes weren't going to feel good to her family members, but it was definitely in their interest as much as it was in my client's interest to allow them to experience these situations. It was in their best interest because my client felt emotionally more stable and less burned out. She was more present for them and better able to help when they needed her. Being more present improved her relationship with her husband, and her children began learning a little about taking care of themselves and being less dependent on her. All adolescents need to learn independence, and by not being there for them all the time, she was fostering their independence. Once she saw that it was in everyone's best interest, saying no and setting boundaries became more manageable for her.

The idea that if you do enough for others you will get what you need in return is a fallacy. If you have this perspective, you probably don't talk about it much—it's an unstated expectation. Have you noticed that it doesn't usually work out that way? If you give to others all the time, you lead them to expect that you are always doing for them. They take it for granted that you don't need anything from them, which is a comfortable way for them to have a relationship with you. Then when you need help, they either don't recognize that you need help or they don't know how to help. They've never had to help you in the past and it feels strange for roles to be reversed. It is not uncommon for relationships to be lost when you need help from people who have never before been asked to help you.

Natural Consequences

Being kind to someone without being nice is not easy to do. Here is where I like to introduce the idea of natural consequences. When parents discipline children, they experience consequences for their behavior. Those consequences are imposed by powerful others. It is nearly impossible in everyday relationships to impose consequences on adults. We can't send them to their rooms or take away privileges in the same way. This is the type of situation where being kind really has power. Remember, being kind is being helpful and caring in a friendly, generous, and considerate manner. It is doing what is in everyone's best interest in a kind, generous, and considerate manner.

Natural consequences include things like
- If a person is rude, hateful, disrespectful, abusive, and so on, other people won't want to interact with them.
- If a driver drives recklessly, they are in an automobile accident.

- If a person overspends, they run out of money at the end of the month.
- If a person stays up all night, they are tired the next day.

Natural consequences apply to everyone, even to partners who are angry and abusive, who cheat on the relationship, and who are emotionally distant, along with a myriad of other dysfunctional ways of relating. Having a conversation about dysfunctional behavior is the right place to start, but if it doesn't result in changed behavior, allowing someone to experience the natural consequences of their behavior is the next logical step. Natural consequences provide feedback about the impact of their behavior in a way that no conversation can and presents them with an opportunity to change. (Of course they won't see it that way, but that isn't your problem.)

A client of mine told a story about her friend, Joan. Joan met Mary through a friend at work. Mary was single and pregnant. After giving birth, she was struggling, so Joan, who had a history of being a single mother like Mary, offered to help. She invited Mary to come live with her, reasoning that if she could help her out, Mary could get on her feet. At first, Mary and the baby seemed happy and healthy but it soon became clear that something wasn't adding up. She neglected the child, didn't help out around the house, and lied about looking for a job. Ultimately, Joan had to make a choice. She didn't want to hurt the baby, but she could no longer support Mary, so she told Mary to move out. She gave Mary several chances to change her behavior and plenty of notice to find new living arrangements, but on the day of the deadline, Mary hadn't made any changes or found a new place to live. Undeterred, Joan kicked her and the baby out of the house.

This is a tough story and it may be hard to see how being hardhearted and sending a mother and her infant to the streets could possibly be in Mary's or the baby's best interest, even though it was in Joan's best interest, but the story has a positive ending. Social services stepped in and Mary was given a place in a group home and help applying for jobs. While she was in the group home, it became clear that Mary was neglecting her child. The state temporarily took the baby away from Mary and a friend of Joan's stepped up to take him in while the state began to teach Mary how to be a better parent. Now the baby is in a stable, loving home and Mary can still visit him. Whether she learns from this and becomes a better parent remains to be seen, but she's been given a chance she wouldn't otherwise have and her son is in a good place. What seemed like a move that would hurt Mary and the baby turned out to be in the best interest of everyone now and into the future.

If you are in a difficult situation and you need to make a decision that seems to hurt another person, consider whether the "hurt" is actually the consequences of their behavior. If so, it is likely that experiencing those consequences is ultimately in their best interest. It gives them a chance to learn something and make better decisions for themselves and others now and into the future.

Nuances of the Rules

The lessons in this book contain a lot of depth and opportunity for nuance, so I encourage you to reread portions as they apply to the situations you are confronting. In this section, I want to discuss some of the more nuanced ways of thinking about the rules.

Let's start with the conflict I mentioned earlier between Rules #2 and #3. If you've practiced these two rules, you have no doubt wondered how to resolve the question of properly labeling someone's behavior and assuming they are doing the best they can.

The way I recommend resolving this conflict gracefully is to give your partner the benefit of the doubt about whether they were doing their best, but make a distinction between giving him the benefit of the doubt and giving him a second (or third or hundredth) chance. It is possible to both accurately label the effect of a person's behavior and to understand that they are doing the best they can with what they have. The two understandings are not mutually exclusive. Just because you understand where someone is coming from or what is driving their behavior, that doesn't mean you have to give them another chance. Once someone has shown you who they are, you should believe that's who they are, even if you know the circumstances that drive their behavior.

Travis and Samantha

Samantha's husband was always late. She had spoken to him several times about how his behavior made her feel and how it looked to others, and Travis acknowledged her points and expressed understanding, but his behavior didn't change. After several discussions, Samantha applied Rules #2 and #3. She realized that Travis's behavior was disrespectful and that he apparently didn't care enough about what she or other people thought to change his behavior. Following Rule #3, she also saw that Travis had little sense of time and didn't respond to her reminders. It was as if he was being a little rebellious. She didn't use her understanding of his behavior to excuse it, but she began to allow him to experience the natural consequences of his lateness. If they had agreed on a time to be at an event and he wasn't ready to leave on time, she took her own car and left him behind. He was naturally angry with Samantha for leaving without him, but after a couple of times and several "discussions," he started paying more attention to the time.

There could have been an alternate ending to this story. Travis could have become rigid in his behavior and refused to respond to the consequences of Samantha's decision to leave without him. The conflict could have revealed other aspects of Travis's psychology and their relationship that were bigger than his chronic lateness, which would be more effective to address than just being late.

When I work with clients around conflicts like this, I point out a simple language tweak that can be quite helpful. The tweak is replacing the word "but" with the word "and." Let's say you have identified that your partner is difficult in a chronic way and has not changed despite your requests. Most women I've worked with in this situation say something to the effect of "He's being intolerable, but I know he's under a lot of pressure." By using the word "but" they negate the fact that his behavior is intolerable. They are left only with the fact that he's under a lot of pressure, as if being under pressure is an excuse for being difficult and should excuse his behavior. If my client instead says, "He's being intolerable and he's under a lot of pressure," that leaves the fact of him being intolerable still on the table. Now it can be addressed.

Being able to make this distinction and hold both ideas at the same time is the beginning of being able to set better boundaries with a person. It also leads nicely into incorporating the remaining rules. Once you are honest with yourself about how a person's behavior affects you, what it says about them, and the reality that they are doing their best or at least meant well, then you will have a better understanding of your own limitations, be able to own and process your emotions, and focus on the present over the past.

In Samantha's case it meant she was honest with herself about how angry and embarrassed she was about Travis's chronic lateness. She realized that he was disrespectful and that it didn't mean enough to him for him to change, and there was something else in his psychology that was hindering his willingness to change and causing him to disregard her. So she worked on making sure she was in the best mental and emotional space possible, she figured out what his behavior meant to her, she identified her emotional reactions, and she processed her emotions outside of her relationship with Travis. Part of that process was to take a look at past situations where she has felt disrespected and examine whether those situations were influencing her reaction to Travis. Then she made a decision to respond to Travis in a different way. She stopped reminding (AKA nagging) him before they were due to leave for an event. Instead, she had a conversation with him first thing in the day about what time she wanted to leave and explained calmly and matter-of-factly that she was tired of arguing with him about being on time and getting angry with him for being late. Therefore, if he was not ready to leave at the appointed time, she was going to leave without him. Of course, he was upset with her for saying she would leave without him, but it didn't seem to affect his ability to be on time, so she left. This made him angrier. He acted out, got angry, and generally behaved like a spoiled child. Samantha had a difficult time withstanding his reactions, but with a little coaching, she got through it. She stood her ground. After a few more instances and "discussions" with Travis after she'd left him at home, he began to be on time more consistently.

The story of Samantha and Travis is a great illustration of applying the rules and being kind in the face of a partner's resistance. There was a conflict between Rules #2 and #3, and identifying and processing her emotional reactions to Travis's lateness didn't change his behavior, so she was left with Rule #7. But in this case being kind wasn't about making everyone feel better; it was about letting Travis experience the natural consequences of his behavior. It didn't feel good in the moment, but in the end the two of them addressed a major issue and it deepened their relationship.

Setting Boundaries Kindly

Setting boundaries is a good skill to learn, but telling people no can feel as if you are being rude or mean if you're not used to it. No, you won't attend the event. No, you won't participate in the bake sale. No, you aren't interested in buying Girl Scout cookies. Usually people who agree to do things they don't want to do reason that it's no big deal. It will earn them points with others. It is expected of them and they don't want to disappoint others. After all, how bad is it that you agreed to buy Girl Scout cookies even though you had recently started a new diet?

It also means not participating in interactions with others who treat you poorly. If the other person violates your rights, you say something. It's not okay, and you aren't going to subject yourself to mistreatment. If the other person persists, you have a decision to make about how (or whether) you are going to participate in the relationship. Telling another person what they did that you don't like is hard. You risk getting into an argument, making them feel bad, or ending the relationship with hard feelings.

For many women, saying no or telling someone to stop mistreating them seems somewhere between hard and impossible. There is a reason it's so hard, and it isn't because women are wimpy people. It's because as young girls, they are heavily rewarded for being agreeable and cooperative. Saying no and setting boundaries that you have to defend by way of a conflict goes against many women's instincts. It's so far outside their skill set, they don't even consider it an option.

If you find yourself in a relationship where you need to stand up for yourself a little more, you need to say no and set an expectation for being treated better, or you have to refuse requests occasionally, effective communication is a good place to start. As a reminder, the formula for effective communication goes something like this:

Talk about the situation. Say something that shows you appreciate the position they are in.

I know you have been looking forward to seeing that movie in the theater on the big screen.

Tell the person how it affects you. Say something about how the situation is impacting you or how you feel about it.

However, I have to work late that night and I won't be able to enjoy the movie after such a long day.

State your request. Ask them to accommodate you in some manner.

Can you please find another day in your calendar that works and let me know?

OR

Could we go on Sunday instead?

As always, you want to keep in mind the principles of effective communication and everyone's rights (including the right to have a negative reaction). It might be a good idea to review effective communication from Rule #1.

Being Kind in Hard Conversations

In Rule #1, I explained how to use effective communication to tell the truth as you see it. That's a great tool for stating your perspective or desires. But sometimes situations call for more than being able to state your case assertively. Often you need to have a whole, hard conversation. How do you conduct the conversation so that all parties leave with their dignity intact? How do you conduct hard conversations in a kind way?

This is tricky. Attempts to soften the blow often muddy the message, and your partner may not understand what you mean, leaving your message effectively undelivered. There are few things more frustrating than telling a person something difficult and being misunderstood. You may resort to being a little too direct just to get your message across, and that doesn't feel good, either.

Your goal is to deliver your message in a way the other person can hear and understand, while telling them something you know they won't want to hear. There is a way to do this. It doesn't guarantee the other person won't be upset, but it's a way to deliver a hard message in a kind way.

I don't have a fancy name for this method, but I think of Mary Poppins every time I use it. The opening line of one of her songs is "A spoon full of sugar helps the medicine go down." That is essentially what this method entails. You are going to tell the person things you like about them before giving them the difficult news.

All conversations start out on a neutral plane and move up and down throughout the conversation. Most of the time we don't think about this, but we've all had conversations where we felt like a bomb had been dropped on us. They end on a negative note. The goal of this method is to end the conversation on a neutral note. You do this by first lifting the other person (and the tone of the conversation) up a few notches. Give the person honest and sincere feedback about what they do well and what you appreciate about them. Then as the conversation progresses tell them what you need to say. These statements will bring the tone back down. The goal is to end at a neutral place.

For example, let's suppose you've decided to end your relationship. There are a lot of good things about the relationship, but enough not-so-good things that you've decided you'd be better off without the relationship, at least the way it is right now. You need out of the relationship and to have distance from your partner. That's a difficult message to deliver as well as to receive. Start the conversation by telling your partner how much you love, respect, and appreciate them and all they do. Talk about things that go well and the importance of their contributions. This brings the tone of the conversation up above neutral. Then shift the conversation to the decision you've made. Talk about your conclusion that the relationship is no longer serving you, and for you it has come to an end. It's time to close the book on the relationship. You need to love them from a different space than from within the relationship. If you do this well, you'll end back at a neutral place.

I have three points about this process. First, it doesn't mean that the other person is necessarily going to agree that the relationship is bad enough to end it. If they did, they may have been the one to say something. It also doesn't mean they are going to walk away feeling warm and fuzzy because you complimented them before delivering your message. But it will leave your partner with some dignity.

Second, provide as few specific details as possible. I'd encourage you to avoid saying things like "Because you yell at me, I can no longer be in the relationship." If you do that, they will likely argue one of two things. Either that they don't yell or that they can reframe yelling in the future. Either way, you've given them something to argue about. Instead, talk about the relationship no longer serving you and your need to be out of the relationship.

Finally, if the person wants to argue with you about whether it's time to end the relationship, I'd encourage you to stick to your concluding points, rather than enter into an argument. A good rebuttal is "Nevertheless, it is time for me to close up this relationship." The key word here is "nevertheless." It's a great way of returning to your point without having to argue your way there. Notice also that you are not asking for agreement. You are kindly asserting your position. It isn't open for debate.

Rule Recap

Rule #7: Above All Else Be Kind

Being kind means being caring and helpful in a gentle, friendly, considerate way.

Being helpful does not always mean you make the person feel better. Sometimes being helpful means allowing a person to experience the natural consequences of their decisions and behavior.

Do what is in everyone's best interest. It is in everyone's best interest if it is good for you, your partner, your family, your community, and society now and on into the future.

When you have to have a difficult conversation, start by being positive and then shift to the difficult message. This should help them hear what you have to say, even though they may still be upset by your message. Try not to provide details, only your conclusion, and if they try to argue with you just return to your main point.

Epilogue

You have chaos in your soul
and lightning in your veins.
You, my dear, were made
for wild, magical things.

~Erin Matlock

MY CLIENTS WANT TO be their best selves. They want to feel good about their relationships and be happy in their lives. Doesn't everyone? If this describes you and if you don't have the quality relationships you want, you have to change something. Following these rules is a change you can make. Although it may seem like a lot to ask, you can start with one rule and later add in a second rule, and so on. If you make this change it will affect not just your relationship with your primary partner, but all your relationships. That's because one of the best side effects of following these rules is the sense of being a stronger, more confident person. Being able and willing to tell yourself the truth and sit with your emotional experiences will keep you in touch with who you are.

You are a loving human who wants to connect. Make sure your connections are good for you. Don't let just anyone into your inner circle of friends or allow just anyone to be emotionally intimate with you. Following the rules will shine a light on your value. You will learn the importance of saying no to people who don't value you.

It is my mission to help others have better relationships. I do this by helping my clients feel empowered and see their value so they can make better choices about who to connect with and how to conduct themselves in a relationship. I wish for you, dear reader, the belief that you are worthy of a great relationship—and the willingness to wait for the right relationship to develop, rather than settling for one you think you can tolerate.

Summary of the Rules

Rule #1: Tell the truth sooner rather than later.

Although there are many reasons to lie, telling the truth is important. The sooner you tell the truth, the better, because the longer a lie goes on, the worse the consequences are when the truth comes out.

Rule #2: When someone shows you who they are, believe them.

Actions speak louder than words. It's more important to pay attention to people's behavior because this says more about their character than their words do.

Rule #3: Always assume the best in your partner.

Assuming the worst is corrosive to a relationship. In the absence of evidence that your partner is not doing his best, assume he is doing the best he can with what he has.

Rule #4: Know your limitations.

Understand which situations and conditions cause you to be compromised physically or emotionally and avoid making relationship decisions or getting into difficult conversations during these times.

Rule #5: Own your emotions.

When you have an unpleasant or difficult emotional reaction, do not blame your partner. Instead, explore your reaction and what it means about you.

Rule #6: The Past Plays a Part, but the Present is Primary

Understand how your past is likely to influence your current behavior and reactions. Know when that is the case and work to keep the negative or inappropriate influences from the past out of your reactions to your current relationship.

Rule #7: Be kind.

Being kind isn't being nice or polite. It is doing what is in the best interest of you and your partner now and into the future.

Acknowledgments

A few years ago I connected with Erin Matlock at a neurofeedback conference. She was giving a talk on using social media to promote clinical work. Since then she has helped me personally and professionally, lifted me up when I needed a lift, and given me direction when I felt lost. She has also pushed me harder than I've been pushed in a long time. Without her encouragement, this book would not have come into being.

Michael Hamilton gave me insight into the power and value of a truly kind and generous man. We laughed together and he let me cry on his shoulder. He encouraged me when I was scared and showed me how to be in the moment. I am always amazed at his creativity and ability to understand others. Plus, he is a great cook. Thank you for everything, Michael!

I met John Mekrut through Erin, and he's been the perfect sounding board for all manner of personal and professional issues. I'm sure there were plenty of times he didn't know what to say, but nonetheless he was perfectly helpful.

Erin also introduced me to Ellen Goodwin and Patricia Faust. Ellen cheered me on through the initial phase of just getting the ideas and words on paper. Patricia became the content editor. They were such good friends and supporters through the process of writing. Ellen kept me writing and Patricia gave me encouragement to keep going when I doubted my work.

Meghan Pinson, my editor, was such a gift from heaven. She was excited about this project and her wonderful feedback was just what I needed to get it off my desk and out into the world.

Kelly Bickel is that once in a lifetime friend who has helped me rise above the trauma and chaos life has thrown at me. We've been friends for 20 years now and she's such a blessing to me.

My three sisters, Elizabeth, Phyllis, and Carolyn, along with my parents, Donald and Patricia, are the ground beneath my feet.

Thank you to Cheryl Wilson, who helped me hone my message and completely understood both the angst and opportunity of being single and free to reinvent myself.

Appendix

To get full-page versions of the following worksheets go to:

www.drjulieshafer.com/7-rules-bonuses

Why Did You Lie Worksheet

Answer these questions when you find that you lied (or you want to lie) but you don't know why, and you want to tell the truth.

1. What is the situation? Write a 2–3 sentence description.

2. What is the lie you told (or want to tell)?

3. What kind of lie did you tell (or want to tell)?
    ❏ Promote yourself? ❏ Protect yourself?
    ❏ To have an impact on others? ❏ Just because?

4. What is the truth?

5. What do you think will happen if you tell the truth?

6. How will telling the truth make you feel in the short term?

7. How will telling the truth make you feel in the long term?

8. What emotional state are (were) you trying to avoid by being deceptive?

9. Are you making any assumptions that may be clouding your expectation of what will happen? What are they?

10. What can you say to challenge your expectation?

Worksheet for Why You Avoid the Truth

Complete this worksheet if you are reluctant to tell the truth about something. If you are doing the worksheet as you read the book, complete Step 1 before moving on to Step 2.

Step 1

1. What is the situation?

2. What do you really want to say? What is your truth?

3. If you told your partner the truth, how do you expect him to respond?

4. If he responds this way, how would you feel?

5. Are you avoiding telling him the truth because you don't want to deal with his response?

Step 2

6. What if he didn't respond in the way you expected? How else might he respond? Think of 2 or 3 different responses, even if you think they are highly unlikely.

7. For each alternate response, write out how that response would make you feel.

Worksheet for Communicating Effectively

This worksheet will help you develop a script for effective communication. There are two parts. The first part helps you figure out how you're feeling and what you believe. The second part helps you create a script you can use to talk with your partner.

1. Describe the situation in 2–3 sentences.

2. What do I want? (What's my truth?)

3. What do I think will happen if I tell the truth? What scares me the most about telling the truth?

4. Will this really happen? If I believe it will, how do I know? *Remember when you are predicting what will happen you are making an assumption.

5. What are my rights in this situation?

6. What are my partner's rights?

In this next part you will create a script for communicating assertively and effectively.

7. What is going on with my partner? What's his situation?

8. How does it affect me? How do I feel about what happened? What do I need?

9. What do I want from my partner? What specific action could my partner take to improve the situation?

10. Using the 3 parts above, write out your script:

List of Emotion Words

Note that words in a column describe similar emotional states.

Pleasant Emotion Words

Open	Happy	Alive	Good
Understanding	Great	Playful	Calm
Confident	Gay	Courageous	Peaceful
Reliable	Joyous	Energetic	At ease
Easy	Lucky	Liberated	Comfortable
Amazed	Fortunate	Optimistic	Pleased
Free	Delighted	Provocative	Encouraged
Sympathetic	Overjoyed	Impulsive	Clever
Interested	Gleeful	Frisky	Surprised
Satisfied	Thankful	Animated	Content
Receptive	Important	Spirited	Quiet
Accepting	Festive	Thrilled	Certain
Kind	Ecstatic	Wonderful	Relaxed
	Glad		Serene
	Cheerful		Free & easy
	Sunny		Bright
	Merry		Blessed
	Elated		Reassured
	Jubilant		
	Satisfied		

More Pleasant Emotion Words

Love	Interested	Positive	Strong
Loving	Concerned	Eager	Impulsive
Considerate	Affected	Keen	Free
Affectionate	Fascinated	Earnest	Sure
Sensitive	Intrigued	Intent	Certain
Tender	Absorbed	Anxious	Rebellious
Devoted	Inquisitive	Inspired	Unique
Attracted	Nosy	Determined	Dynamic
Passionate	Snoopy	Excited	Tenacious
Admiration	Engrossed	Enthusiastic	Hardy
Warm	Curious	Bold	Secure
Touched		Brave	
Sympathy		Daring	
Close		Challenged	
Loved		Optimistic	
Comforted		Re-enforced	
Drawn to		Confident	
		Hopeful	

LOVED

Unpleasant Emotion Words

Angry	Depressed	Confused	Helpless
Irritated	Lousy	Upset	Incapable
Enraged	Disappointed	Doubtful	Alone
Hostile	Discouraged	Uncertain	Anxious
Insulting	Ashamed	Indecisive	Paralyzed
Sore	Powerless	Perplexed	Fatigued
Annoyed	Diminished	Embarrassed	Useless
Upset	Guilty	Hesitant	Inferior
Hateful	Dissatisfied	Shy	Vulnerable
Unpleasant	Miserable	Stupefied	Empty
Offensive	Detestable	Disillusioned	Forced
Bitter	Repugnant	Unbelieving	Hesitant
Aggressive	Despicable	Skeptical	Despair
Resentful	Disgusting	Distrustful	Frustrated
Inflamed	Abominable	Misgiving	Distressed
Provoked	Terrible	Lost	Woeful
Incensed	Despair	Unsure	Pathetic
Infuriated	Sulky	Uneasy	Tragic
Cross	Bad	Pessimistic	In a stew
Worked up	A sense of	Tense	Dominated
Boiling	loss	At a loss	
Fuming	Weary		
Indignant			

More Unpleasant Emotion Words

Indifferent	Afraid	Hurt	Sad
Insensitive	Fearful	Crushed	Tearful
Dull	Terrified	Tormented	Sorrowful
Nonchalant	Suspicious	Deprived	Pained
Neutral	Anxious	Pained	Grief
Reserved	Alarmed	Tortured	Anguish
Weary	Panic	Dejected	Desolate
Bored	Nervous	Rejected	Desperate
Preoccupied	Scared	Injured	Pessimistic
Cold	Worried	Offended	Unhappy
Disinterested	Frightened	Afflicted	Lonely
Lifeless	Timid	Aching	Grieved
	Shaky	Victimized	Mournful
	Restless	Heartbroken	Dismayed
	Doubtful	Agonized	
	Threatened	Appalled	
	Cowardly	Humiliated	
	Quaking	Wronged	
	Menaced	Alienated	
	Wary	Embarrassed	

Identifying and Processing Emotional Triggers

Complete this worksheet each time you are triggered. Over time you will begin to see patterns in your reactions.

Date: _____

1. What happened? Describe it in 2–3 sentences.

2. What was your emotional reaction?

3. Was your reaction bigger or different than others (or you) expected? How so?

4. What other situations have created this feeling in the past?

5. Based on your answers to the previous 2 questions, what is the type of condition(s) that usually cause you to feel this way?

6. What do you tell yourself about feeling this way? For example, "I'm unlovable" or "It's his fault."

7. Was this one of those times that feeing this way (and having those thoughts) got in the way of having a peaceful and close relationship? Why or why not?

8. If your reaction got in the way, what could you do differently next time?

Processing Emotions Worksheet

Use this worksheet to process difficult emotions. This is a way to work through emotional reactions so you don't take them out on your partner.

Date:_____

1. What was the situation? Describe in 2–3 sentences.

2. How did I feel about the situation? List 3–10 emotions from the Emotion Words list or add emotions of your own.

3. What are my thoughts about the situation?

4. Do you feel this way at other times? If so, what other situations create this feeling?

5. What do I tell myself about feeling this way? For example, "I'm unlovable" or "It's his fault."

6. Is what you tell yourself the truth? Yes/No

7. If it isn't the truth, what is the truth? What else could you tell yourself about the situation?

8. If you believed your answer to the previous question, how would you feel about the situation?

Transcript
A Breathing Exercise for Emotional Overwhelm

Sit in a comfortable chair with your feet on the floor, your back supported by the back of the chair or sofa, and your hands resting comfortably in your lap.

Close your eyes and listen to my voice.

You recently experienced a feeling of being emotionally overwhelmed.

Think of what happened and how it made you feel.

Focus on the sensations that happen in your body when you recreate your emotional reaction to what just happened.

You want to recreate how it felt in your body as much as possible.

You may feel something in your throat or chest or abdomen.

You may feel tightness, heat, a sinking feeling, a pulse, a tingle, or something you can't quite describe.

As you focus on the bodily sensations, start to take slow, deep breaths, in and out.

Breathe into your belly, slowly and deeply.

Allow your breath to lightly brush up against that bodily sensation and notice what happens.

Does the sensation change in intensity, move to another place, come and go with your breath?

Keep taking slow, deep breaths.

If the sensation moves, focus on the new place it went to.

If the sensation starts to diminish, allow it to go.

Now that you have taken several slow deep breaths, reflect on how you feel.

Notice that you focused intensely on your feelings and learned to be with them. They didn't hurt you, although they were unpleasant.

When you are ready, open your eyes.

✽ ✽ ✽

If you do this exercise when you get emotionally overwhelmed, you will find that your emotional reactions are less overwhelming. You will still be upset by difficult situations, but you will be able to think and consider how to respond, rather than getting overwhelmed and being at the mercy of your reaction.

Abusive Relationship Resources

This is a list of a few online resources that describe abusive behavior and how to get help.

WebMD, an article on the signs of domestic abuse: https://www.webmd.com/mental-health/mental-domestic-abuse-signs

This article from POPSUGAR in Australia gives advice on what to do if someone you know is in an abusive relationship: https://www.popsugar.com.au/news/How-Tell-Someone-Victim-Domestic-Violence-43621304

National Domestic Violence Hotline in the US: https://www.thehotline.org/

Domestic abuse hotlines and resources in Australia: https://www.whiteribbon.org.au/find-help/domestic-violence-hotlines/

Domestic abuse help in the UK: http://www.nationaldomesticviolencehelpline.org.uk/

Domestic abuse hotlines and resources across Canada: http://endingviolencecanada.org/getting-help/

Patricia Evans has written several books on verbal abuse, including The Verbally Abusive Relationship and Victory over Verbal Abuse, among others.

Below are two podcasts that describe controlling and manipulative behavior quite well. **Note that both these podcasts graphically depict people being mistreated and may be triggering.

- Dirty John – A story about man who manipulates his way into the life of a woman and her family

- Real Crime Profile – A retired FBI Agent/Profiler, a criminal behavioral specialist, and the casting director for CBS' Criminal Minds profile behavior from real criminal cases.

A playlist of TED Talks that discuss domestic violence: https://blog.ted.com/5-brave-personal-stories-of-domestic-abuse/

Glossary

<u>Accountability</u>: to assess your behavior and then find ways of being or doing better next time. Accountability is telling the truth about your behavior without unwarranted criticism.

<u>Confirmation bias</u>: the phenomenon of seeing what you expect to see.

<u>Criticism</u>: finding fault, judging, or labeling yourself or others.

<u>Emotional resilience</u>: the ability to adapt to stressful situations and "roll with the punches." Emotional resilience allows you to keep your emotions in check, take in what's happening, and be flexible.

<u>Kindness</u> (to be kind): kindness is expressing caring and helpfulness in a way that is gentle, friendly, generous, and considerate.

<u>Red flags</u>: those behaviors that in hindsight were signs that something wasn't right with the person or the relationship.

<u>Self-signaling</u>: to judge yourself based on how you behave.

<u>Social norms</u>: unstated expectations about how to behave in social situations.

<u>Successive approximation</u>: getting closer and closer to what you want with each new behavior.

Thank You!

Thank you for taking the time to read this book. I hope you get something out of it helpful for you and your relationship.

If you'd be interested in connecting with me you can follow me on Facebook:

https://www.facebook.com/JulieShaferPhD/

You can also send me message through my website:

www.drjulieshafer.com/contact/

Be Loved and Be Well,

39590480R00132

Made in the USA
Middletown, DE
18 March 2019